BELLROCK

JOHN MOSS
BELLROCK

NC Press Limited
Toronto, 1983

Cover Painting: Ruth Brooks
Cover Photograph: Virginia Moss
Typesetting: Jay Tee Graphics Ltd.
Cover design: Don Fernley

Canadian Cataloguing in Publication Data
Moss, John, 1940-
 Bellrock
ISBN 0-919601-83-9

1. Moss, John, 1940- 2. Critics - Canada -
Biography. I. Title.
PS8025.M6A33   C818'.5403   C83-098767-3
PR9183.M6A33

1,290

We would like to thank the Ontario Arts Council and the Canada
Council for their assistance in the production of this book. Congratulations to the
Ontario Arts Council on its 20th anniversary.

New Canada Publications, a division of NC Press Limited, Box 4010,
Station A, Toronto, Ontario, M5W 1H8.

Printed in Canada

Contents

BELLROCK

the shortest distance between 2 points
on a revolving circumference
is a curved line
— Gwendolyn MacEwan

*Tout ceci doit être consideré comme
dit par un personnage de roman
— Roland Barthes*

Saturday, September 3, 1977

one

Bellrock is on the Depot Creek branch of the Napanee River, twenty-five miles north of Kingston, Ontario, three thousand miles away from Vancouver.

Bellrock is a village on the lower edge of the Canadian Shield, where it sweeps down almost to Lake Ontario. It is also an island in the middle of the mill pond at the edge of the village, and it is a house we have built there, from the remains of an old log farmhouse. The house is set close to the water on the side of the island away from the village. The water is slow and brown, but deep and clean to drink or swim in. In the cold night air of winter its residual warmth makes the ice crack periodically with a piercing moan.

Bellrock is a dream I share with Ginny and with Julie and Laura, one I'm moving away from and deeper into, leaving them behind to drive alone across the continent.

[15]

This is about Bellrock. Words arranged as I drive.

I intended to work on a novel using my tape recorder, but I've been on the road an hour now and already fiction is impossible.

Moving away, memories and perception are vivid but the words are slow to come. Beginnings are the most difficult.

Dreams cost, and we've run out of money. There's a job waiting for me in Vancouver, at the University of British Columbia. Ginny and the kids will join me when they can, in a couple of months if all goes well. In the spring we'll return to Bellrock.

• • •

Now three hours from home, on the same route Ginny took in the summer to Port Carling, riding her bike to the cottage. There's a bit of autumn in the leaves now. This would have been her third day, riding.

Ginny bikes, and the kids and I ride horses. We have a palomino mare called Lady, fifteen years old and fifteen hands tall; and we have Troy, a big chestnut hunter, a gelding. The horses are part of the dream. So is Paddy. He's an Irish Wolfhound, the second tallest dog in the world. Paddy, personally. Standing upright with his forepaws resting on my shoulders he clears seven feet. Paddy is lean and grey, with haunting eyes, but he smiles a lot. We call him Killer sometimes but it doesn't take.

[16]

By dream I don't mean fantasy, not unreal and not unattainable. Impractical perhaps but within reach and need. A dream to live within.

Haliburton, a huge hill sloping into the town centre. Four hours now. The kids and I tried not to cry when I left them with Ginny under the ironwood tree in the pasture. We said things desperately, then, whispering urgently and the words didn't matter, holding each other, shuddering against the unfamiliar emotion of saying goodbye for a long time, uncertain time. Julie is ten and Laurie is seven. Ginny didn't cry. This will be the longest we've been apart. The strain showed. Even when we were separated for six months, on the verge of divorce nearly a decade ago, we saw each other often.

Bellrock is our form of survival.

We want this. Not the separation, which is necessary to sustain the dream, but the dream itself.

When we made the move to Bellrock, to a half-built log house on our own small island, we had no idea what the real demands of our commitment were. I think we didn't want to know. I resigned my teaching job in Montreal. Ginny was just finishing her Ph.D. in psychology at McGill and had lined up part-time research work at Queen's, in Kingston. From the sale of our Montreal house we made enough to carry us for a while. It was not enough to last. Bellrock was never planned as a minimal facility back-to-the-earth experiment. We wanted a comfortable home in the country; we wanted to be free of mortgage and debts, to modestly indulge our saner whims. To live well.

We wanted to make our own home with our own hands, to have a blue bidet, to eat wild asparagas, to keep bees, have horses, raise a garden, live within the world and not apart from it as we had seemed to do in Montreal, where the stars are drowned by streetlights and the weather comes over the radio.

We had lived too much between memory and anticipation, as if life were a run-through, a rehearsal for the real thing.

Moving.

I'll be in Port Carling in another hour. Probably what I'll do is drive down to the dock where Whitings used to be, when I spent my summers at the cottage across the bay. There were racks and racks of comic books in Whitings. Clear-drawn strips of ducks who talked inside my head, Huey, Dewey, Louie, all different voices, each one mine. Little Big Books; furred at the corner from making pictures move across the pages as you flipped them with your thumb. Plastic Man, Lone Ranger, Red Ryder. I was L'il Beaver, Tonto, Plastic Man's Chinese sidekick, what's his name, I can hear and see him vividly; Kato? I was a second-oldest child. For a whole summer in Port Carling I was Robin. I read Wonder Woman, Superman, the Blackhawks, they follow in a sequence. Before them, a prolonged Captain Marvel phase. Captain Marvel Junior, the crippled newsboy Billy Batson after he said "Captain Marvel." Captain Marvel had to say "Shazam." I don't remember what Mary Marvel said or who she was before she said it. She had black hair. She had long smooth legs, little skirts, no crotch.

I read Classics Comics assiduously.

I drive for long quiet stretches, hardly thinking in words at all. Images; flipping by.

In 1951 Princess Elizabeth passed through Canada.

We waited to see her, Richard and I, with Mom I think, for hours and hours at the Dundas train station outside Hamilton. I was eleven. A woman behind me in the waiting crowd pressed sharp hard lumps against my upper back. Breasts. For hours and hours I kept them there, fiddling with my box camera, standing tall, afraid of losing her. So busy with my camera when the Royal train passed through I missed seeing anything at all except the train, receding. On the photograph the Royals were blurred and small, an imperfection.

[18]

Where Whitings was, there's now a government wharf. You can see the cottage, post-card sized across the water. Rambling, verandahed (since 1911 host to six generations of us, overlapping). Even from here there's a shabby elegance about the cottage, storied high over the shore line beyond the two-slip boathouse, one slip for the launch and one slip dry for rowboat and canoes. Between the cottage and the boathouse and on up the hillside are towering pines, and the soft scent of pine needles generations deep and the sweet smell of the singing grass on hot summer days; liquid tinkling sounds of water in the evening lapping against the boathouse timbers; moonlight filling the bay across to Port, a few lights in town around Whitings and the Boat Works; a full sky.

I can remember hearing Churchill at the cottage, with Grammy and Aunt Beth and Mom. I think I can remember, the images are there. Dad was Overseas. I think I can remember, but maybe they're other peoples' memories I've picked up on over the years.

I remember Aunt Beth meeting us in the launch late at night, after we flashed our headlights across the bay. That was before the road or telephone.

I remember arriving different times, and I vividly remember leaving, though each summer's leaving blends into the memory of the next. I don't remember visiting but being there, and being pretty much on my own. If Rich was up at the same time . . . he was older. He had a friend. Steve was five years younger, a World War between us. I was six or seven when Liz was born and nine when Erry came along.

At the centre is the memory of my grandmother, standing at the corner of the verandah, waving as the launch surged into power, ending my summers. This is a fixture in my mind, her one ancient hand on the wooden railing, and the other waving the handkerchief that she usually kept tucked up her sleeve, calling goodbye over the roar of the motor, over the distance between us.

[19]

She did the same for all of us, but knowing it wasn't just for you made it somehow better, a bond between you and the others, you and the place. Continuity; ritual. Her eyes were nearly crying, always smiling, lips moving, moving now it almost seems.

Each summer the same. At fourteen I worked at a fruit stand and always worked at something after that, Army Cadets at Ipperwash, Camp Counsellor at Camp Temagami, bus driver, bush guide; but always I stopped in, even for a day or two, each summer.

In midsummer of 1968 Ginny and Julie and I, Laurie wasn't born yet, drove up through Algonquin Park from Kingston and back down into Muskoka, to Port Carling. This was eight months after Grammy's hundredth birthday. Erry met us at the end of the road to tell us Grammy was in the hospital in Bracebridge.

I went into the room alone. It was hot and quiet, late in the afternoon. Grammy looked uncomfortable and out of place. She was partially paralysed, on intravenous, surrounded by arcane machinery. Her teeth were taken out; not the front ones, they were still her own, her pride. The blinds were down. I had been told not to expect too much, but when I clasped her hand she responded. I talked to her, and the next day I held her hand and talked to her, the two of us alone in the darkened room. And the next day I talked to her and told her we had to go back to Kingston, Ginny and I with the baby. She knew we'd been separated, although everyone had kept it from her. Grammy squeezed my hand so it hurt and she looked into me, reassuring and comforting. We kissed goodbye.

I walked to the door and turned around. She drew herself up from the bedclothes and with a fresh white handkerchief from her sleeve waved me out of the room.

She died a week later. When I go back now to Port Carling, I sometimes hear the broken planes of her aging voice in the sounds of the boathouse, calling an eight or a ten or a twelve-year-old to come right up for cake and Cambrick tea.

Driving.

Between Bracebridge and Port Carling. I've only gone two hundred miles and I'm exhausted. I've got to do at least another three hundred today or I'll never get there. It's slow going, like driving through vaseline.

Building Bellrock:

Much of the work was done by hand. The design evolved out of what we had to work with and what we discovered we could do and, most of all, from what we dreamed it to be. It is a place at home in its natural setting, wholly an expression of our lives together during the years we've been building it.

Bellrock, Ginny and the kids; Bellrock is a code for all I'm leaving and a code-word too for the gap that's opening up between us. . . .

My mind keeps slipping off to other things, surrogate feelings I can cope with, childhood memories, my grandmother, things she told me, stories without beginnings or endings, stories that are instantaneous in my head unless I give them words; then they separate from me, become artifacts.

The first summer after Ginny and I were married I taught in a penitentiary, Collins Bay, medium to maximum security. Everyone on the staff wore close-clipped mustaches and service ribbons on their uniforms, like commissionaires. I didn't identify with the convicts either. I felt their anger sometimes, anger and fear, and sometimes their abject desolation. . . . I have nightmares still that leave me empty, grasping, feeling utterly exposed. Prison memories.

On my last day at the pen my group had a party, a couple of bottles of contraband scotch. I drank enough to show how pleased I was, but I

[21]

didn't get drunk. I should have. One day on the street in Toronto I bumped into one of the guys, but he didn't recognize me.

Port Carling sign, the village limits. A couple of miles until I'm actually there. Still travelling known territory!

• • •

Just pulled onto Highway 69, on my way to Parry Sound. Next Sudbury, then Sault Ste. Marie. Port Carling behind me.

When I came over the hill in Port, driving down towards the swing bridge, I caught a glimpse of the cottage across the bay, saw enough to know people are there, the boathouse doors were open: cousins, children of my mother's nieces and nephews whom I hardly know and haven't seen since Grammy's funeral.

Slowed to a crawl over the bridge. An old man, retired as the lockmaster even when I was a kid, leaned by the side of the bridge, as if waiting for something to happen. I nodded to him but he didn't see me. It's a new bridge, machine operated but redundant since no vessels travel the Muskoka Lakes anymore that can't be handled by the smaller locks on the river. I wish I could remember the old man's name.

I didn't stop.

So far I've been cutting diagonally cross-country. Now I'm on the main route; rolling along. I play with the tape recorder on the seat beside me, without looking at it. I flick it on and off and on, playback, listening to the highway humming in the pauses, behind the words a rushing sound. Nearly silent blips where I've switched off each time; punctuation, a different syntax. Time, reduced to the linear; duration, meaningless.

Ginny and the kids will be eating by now. Right now. Sipping dandelion wine. Ginny's been making it since before I knew her. She has some that's seventeen years old, that fills the mouth and innundates the senses with the merest sip. All the years that it's been working are in each sip, and so is the care in its making and the trust in its future, its eventual fine quality.

I can probably drive for another six hours. By then, even if they stay up late the kids will be in bed, for sure, sound asleep. Ginny too, by then.

It's disturbing to see the painted rock faces along the road, paint neatly covering last year's graffiti. Government agents must come along here every season, effectively marking the best places for next year.

I wonder if graffiti writers return like migrant birds year after year to the same rocks?

Bellrock. Perhaps it will last a generation or two, or perhaps even more. The island itself is changing. It wasn't there two hundred years ago, not until they dammed the river for the mill. By the time the kids are grown the dense pines will have given way to a fine stand of hardwoods, mostly sugar maples but with a few mountain and red maples mixed in. They're already forcing their way up through the pines, reaching for sunlight. I'll never see that time, but I can see it coming. There's one great maple on the island now, there before the pines, spreading over and around the house, inseparable from it.

When you build something, you know that it will change and one day perish, and you do it anyway. You take more care, not less, knowing this.

The walls in the downstairs bathroom with the shower and sauna are done in diagonal cedar strips — it took a month of cutting with a saw and a plane and sometimes a knife, shaping the wood to a fine tolerance until the walls looked soft and warm and beautiful, hardly an effort apparent, the handiwork merged with the wood, the corners and crannies and wood all of a piece. The room doesn't just contain space but shares it. There is satisfaction in that.

Someday it will all be gone. Burnt. Torn down or collapsed with time, indifference. Creation is grievous; consciousness of creation the only compensation.

The ruins that became our house once stood high on a hillside over near Croyden, fourteen miles away. Crumbling, roofless, dessicated, behind a pall of renegade lilacs, the ghosts not gone, but settled, merged with the wasting remains. We bought what there was, marked the beams, the logs, dismantled them, carted them, floated them over, rebuilt, and built onto them to double the size.

As we worked, the work of other lives and earlier times emerged in the axe marks and adze marks on the logs and in the remnants of ox-blood paint on the beams, in the nail holes and the worn spots and in the shapes drawn out of the ancient wood as we put it back to use. We felt the lives of those others, even as it became more and more our own.

Possibly seventy years passed between the emergence of the island above the waters of Depot Creek and the time the pines were planted.

Someone makes the effort to match the cover-up paint with the colour of the rocks. Black on slate grey. Pink on feldspar. Yellow ochre on limestone and granite, garish in the slanting sunlight.

Today is over, almost. Pitch dark now, rainy. Sault Ste. Marie in half an hour. Find a motel room, get a good night's sleep.

It's the darkness, the quiet . . . as evening closed around me, I felt increasingly empty; heavy, contained by the car, rushing nowhere. Laurie, smiling; Julie, pigtails and hugs; Ginny. Love is a hard word to say out loud, alone. Love. Sounds interrogative. Short and mournful. Love and death, alien to the machine. Death hushes, tongue kissing teeth. Easier to say than love.

● ● ●

I miss them so much it frightens me.

It's the anticipation that's got me down, the dread of how much more I'm going to miss them.

So what is Bellrock? That's what I started with today. I go farther and farther into the darkness, deeper and deeper; it remains the centre.

Ginny's Bellrock is not the same as mine, nor Julie's nor Laurie's. Separate even in our dreams, ultimately.

It's been a long day.

The first day. A fragment.

two

Sunday morning; my second day. On highway 17 above Sault Ste. Marie. The sky, the pavement, everything is silvered with a fine rain. Lake Superior shimmers expansively; bush on the right displays luxuriant wetness, not dismal but not inviting either. The highway cuts due north, through wilderness, between bush and water.

Words play through the mind, driving like this. Words separate from meaning, become sounds in the mind, pure as the cries of a wild thing. Impersonal.

What I felt last night, line of pain extending through the darkness back to Bellrock, has snapped this morning with the light of day and a good night's sleep behind me. Now, the heart-beat slapping of the wipers underscores a gnawing urgency that spreads in waves, I'm losing everything to words, hiding in words, avoiding, obscuring. . . .

What I left is now within
Julie Clare Zillah
Laura Frances Errington
My experience of myself with them
Ginny   our shared experience
Bellrock

Last night, for the last five or six hours of driving in the dark, images of the Sudbury evening stayed in mind to haunt me; deep shadows all around, but the sunlight high overhead livid in the spuming smog; driving into the setting sun, into darkness.

And this morning, waves rolling gently in to shore beneath a weight of rain, the wet bush pristine, primeval, at the highway's edge. Time spreads around me, occupies space.

I pass the occasional lodge or camp. It's only September 4th but they're already closed for the season.

Wait ten months for two.

That's the way it was with Bellrock, at first. Not there except when we were. But gradually it took on a life of its own. We'd go there and work on the stone fireplace, the logs, windows, roofing, and then we'd go away and it would be substantial there, waiting incomplete. Like a secret. A vacuum grew between us, wherever we were, from one summer to the next.

After our first summer in Bellrock we lived in Fredericton for three years: tree-lined streets like aisles through a forest subdued by good taste; fine old clapboard houses, subtle-hued with many colours; the great Saint John and the steep walls of the river valley. I loved New

[28]

Brunswick and living in the Maritimes, an hour's drive from the sea — only the Atlantic spawns such familiarity, to be called the "sea." I doubt that I will ever greet the Pacific on such familiar terms.

Next we lived in Montreal for three years; downtown, in Lower Westmount, in a corner house. I could reach my work at Sir George Williams University and Ginny could get to McGill, both in fifteen minutes. Everything we needed was close at hand; stores just up the street, the bank a block away, a park six blocks distant, well-lit at night and guarded.

Then to Bellrock.

I've made it over the hill now, we have, the car and I, it. This it, the Volvo, 145 SL, 1974. Yellow. Station Wagon. Flowing along just fine now. One more mile gone by. 602.4 miles behind me, about 2400 to go. Up and over another hill. A smaller hill. I'm on the down side now, coasting. If all goes well, in a few days I'll be 602.4 miles from Vancouver, looking back on 2400 miles behind me to Bellrock.

In many parts of the country these hills would qualify as mountains. The car keeps to forty-five, that's it, no faster. Not until we're over the top.

Last Thursday I took the car to the garage in Verona for a quick tune-up and oil change. When I went back for it Friday afternoon, Jim, the mechanic, said I was running on two cylinders. He gave me fifty-fifty odds on making Vancouver. Not much better on getting home to Bellrock, three miles away.

Bellrock. Is an unincorporated village of sixty-some persons, many of whom work in Kingston. A century ago there were six operating mills and a cheese factory. There was a school, now used for euchre nights in winter and an annual pot-luck supper. The church has been duplexed. There's still a general store, the heart and crossroads of the village. One mill remains. They made cheese boxes there when we first came to Bellrock, and sawed boards and squared timbers, all by water power, the water level in the pond around our island falling during the workday, making the island bigger, and rising to restore our boundaries overnight. Some of the water spills over the falls and some, channells through a short mill-race, then flume, then wheels, then sluice, meets the main flow again below and continues, joining other streams to become a river for a while, the clean brown water gradually turning murky as it rambles towards Napanee where it meets with Lake Ontario and drifts towards the sea.

The mill was closed down. It is now being restored. Much local history lies between these two events, less than a decade apart.

Apparently no one has determined the criteria for restoration — what period, what degree of historical authenticity. As a working mill it was the accumulation of many periods, different times.

A palisade was recently built around the mill grounds, an expensive fence of sharpened verticle poles machined to similarity, pointed by a giant pencil sharpener, set side by side, admitting only slivers of light. Someone who had never been a kid thought it would keep the village kids out. It does in fact protect them from being surprised by grown-ups while they're in there, smoking or whatever.

Bellrock is small but its founders were not without ambition. It is laid out on a grid pattern, set alongside the main highway from Verona to Enterprise. Old maps and town plans indicate streets that now would pass across fields and over lawns, through living rooms and bedrooms.

Six mills, a church, a school, a store, two stores, a cheese factory — which is now the drive shed beside my mother-in-law's place. Her house was a store for awhile, and a school; now it is a summer place where the generations of her family, Enid's family, get together most Sunday afternoons through the summer, spring and fall, occasionally in the winter.

The village extends away from the south-west corner of the pond, which covers perhaps eight to twelve acres, depending on whether you count the inlets and crannies, the backwaters and marshy edges here and there. It's surprisingly deep in places; the marshy parts are to the east and north, upstream. In the middle of the pond is an island called, on the old maps, Goose Island. From the village you can't tell it's an island; from almost every perspective, it seems a piece with the far shore.

The village is split half and half between newcomers and people who have been there for generations, related one to another two and three times over, mostly Free Methodists or fellow travellers, generally reserved, polite if circumstances demand, drawn easily into conversation only by tragedy or scandal.

Bellrock: for us the village is only at the edge of the word's meaning.

Occasionally something of the-past, an iron hinge rusting in an arbitrary stone-pile encountered on a walk, or a hand-forged door hook on a pantry door, or a rotting beam among the grass in early spring, speaks of other times, separates us from the past. And connects.

In some ways people were less isolated a hundred years ago than now, in such a place. People needed one another for survival and out of that need came community, kinship beyond blood. The village was more self-contained, the farms were literally closer together. Between present day farms, now well into their second century, there once were other farms. There were more people. Generations living together; on the farms, in the villages.

Only one farm in three is worked now, usually on a part-time basis, operated by penitentiary guards or professors or workers from the aluminum or nylon plants in Kingston.

The kids are hauled great distances by bus to district schools.

I went to a two-room school in the village of Blair, near Preston, Waterloo County, sixty miles west of Toronto. Ginny attended a smalltown school in Beeton, sixty miles north of Toronto. Our kids are missing the school-house experience, although there's much to be said for district schools. There was something special, though, having a bunch of kids at different levels all together — I can still name every one of them, all grades and ages, in a school picture, black and white memories, Miss Moore and Mrs. E. Sue King.

[31]

Julie and Laurie go by school-bus to Verona.

Prince Charles Public School. Mr. Sproule. Snowshoeing in winter (someone travels from school to school with snowshoes and takes the kids out back across the tracks and through the woods); workouts on a travelling trampoline; canoeing in the spring. The kids play outside at noon and recess — in trees and grass and country mud.

Closing the village schools didn't kill the smaller communities, but it was a sure sign of their dying — or of their metamorphoses into crossroad satellites of larger centres.

Bellrock is on the rim of the Canadian Shield. At the south edge of the village lies a huge swamp with a corduroy road running through it, flooded half the year, dead straight except for a single dog-leg in the middle. When you emerge from the swamp on the far side, you confront a landscape that is entirely different from what you left behind on the shield, a mile back. The fields are smooth and rich, farm buildings are painted and in good repair. The roads are neatly laid upon the land, not forced erratically among rock outcroppings and undisciplined waterways.

The austere Bellrock landscape,

it took getting used to. I grew up in the fertile rolling farmland of Southwestern Ontario, where a hundred acres can still support a family in style. Around Bellrock, five hundred may not be enough, even with additional acreage leased for pasture.

I just drove under the wingspread of an improbably gigantic Canada Goose! When I started seeing signs for Wawa, thirty or forty miles back, with its Canada Goose logo, I felt vaguely disappointed that I'd miss the main attraction — but I didn't want to take the time. As it turned out, the Wawa Goose overlooks the Trans-Canada. Passing underneath I felt a twinge of satisfaction. It makes up for missing the giant nickel standing on its edge in Sudbury.

I think I'm ready to face the giant sturgeon at Kenora. If it's near the highway.

"Moose crossing." I'm getting north for sure.

The air on the down-wind side of Wawa is choke-filled with sulphur.

Like the smell of the water in Blair when I was a kid: rotten eggs and stale coffee grounds. Some people in that corner of Waterloo County spent thousands drilling for sulphur water. Turn-of-the-century Preston was renowned for its mineral springs. We found it without trying. Mom and Dad designed and built a lovely white brick house high on a hill overlooking the Grand River flats during the Depression. They had to drill deep for water; and then we had to live with it. Sulphur water is esteemed as a palliative and elixir, but it's none too pleasant to the nose or tongue. We got used to it, of course, but each time we'd come back from being away we'd have to get used to it all over again. Guests seldom did.

The Depot Creek branch of the Napanee River has only odourless minerals; the full clean amber smell of water laden with natural sediment, earth and minute vegetation particles.

The river system we're on extends through a series of lakes rather unimaginatively called Fifth Depot, Fourth Depot, Third Depot, Second Depot and First Depot. They are linked by the Depot Creek or the Depot River, which in the middle of the great swamp below us merges with the Napanee.

As the water flows by Bellrock it is brown and clean, though not clear. It's pristine. I wish I could say "pellucid." Out loud, "pellucid," feels good in the mouth — but the river is pristine, meandering toward us and away.

It tests perfectly safe to drink.

When we installed the plumbing last fall we put in a complex filtration system complete with a chlorinator, sand and gravel filter, two hundred gallon holding tank, and a maze of pipes going every which way. We still haven't connected the chlorinator. Maybe someday we'll have to get a drilling rig over on the ice and drill a well. Not yet, though, not for a while.

[33]

Past Sault Ste. Marie the hardwoods were touched by early autumn. Now the highway is hedged by poplars and evergreens and the season is indeterminate.

Just passed a sign announcing gas and a telephone up ahead. When we were kids driving to the cabin in Temagami, I remember we marked off our progress by the changing signs. Somewhere north of Barrie, around Leacock's Orillia, signs for lodging would announce hot and cold running water. A little farther north, just running water. Nothing could be taken for granted. By North Bay the tourist cabins would boast "conveniences" or, more simply, "toilets." Past North Bay the signs were terse, offering only a name, usually Disneyesque. That was along Old Highway 11, Yonge Street, running from downtown Toronto, infinitely north.

From Blair to Temagami was a long exhausting trip, over three hundred miles on bad roads, but always we would rise to exhilaration at the end, arriving four miles up the Northeast Arm on our small island; or arriving back in Blair, high on our hill over the village and the Grand River flats.

The island in Temagami was no more than an acre, solitary, far from shore, windswept: a few gaunt and aging pines, thick scrub brush and bare rocks, blueberry bushes, a flag pole. The cabin was made of logs, with a fieldstone fireplace, moose head, vaulted ceiling, lean-to kitchen, an underground cooler packed around with moss, and a privy down a short path with a box of chemical and a spoon beside the seat and a blow-up on the back of the door of my brother Steve shooting a bow. The cabin had been built by Austin Moss, my father's father, who died before I was born, and Ernie Smith, an Indian who later founded the Temagami Canoe Company, in which my grandfather had an interest. Ernie was part Indian. His wife was Indian. My knowledge of Indians has been filtered through my early experiences with Ernie and Mrs. Smith. She was quiet. She's dead now. Ernie was gregarious. I haven't seen him in years. One summer Ernie took Rich and me into the bush; we killed a moose and told stories in the tent at night, sang "Macnamara's Band", ate loon's eggs, reminisced. I wasn't ten yet.

Ernie is a spinner of tales, mostly featuring himself, some true. Outrageous stories of capturing a tiger escaped from the Havana Zoo (or a leopard, or a lion); trapping the elusive wolverine without a mark on it for the Royal Ontario Museum; organizing Inuit work parties in a series of Arctic expeditions (we called them Eskimos then); discovering ancient Indian cave drawings near Temagami; owning claims on land worked by Temagami Mining. Anything that could be checked out proved true. He did own a small farm in Cuba — though whether it was a reward is hard to say. He did retire with money apparently from the Mine. He does speak Inuit dialects — I think; I'm not sure, not speaking any myself.

My sisters were too young to know Ernie. My parents sold the island when I was about thirteen. Steve went on his own trip with Ernie.

My father visited Bellrock, briefly, two years ago. He reminded me of how much our place had in common with what he called, from his perspective, "ours," in Temagami. I resented the connection. I remember saying something foolish. To hurt him.

He sold his island. Bellrock is not a possession, not mine to sell.

I know the time will come, Julie and Laurie will move away, even lose affection for it. Resent it, maybe, or us. If that happens, I hope eventually they'll rediscover Bellrock, realize how important it is to have some place you can hold in your mind that tells you who you are, where you're from.

I flip on the radio periodically as I approach a town, separated by great distances from one another along the way. I have trouble bringing in very much.

The White River station must be one of the weakest. Four or five miles beyond the town, the signal died out completely, another little oasis of sound fading behind me as I move on through the rain and the bush-desert of Northern Ontario.

The trees now are mostly tamarack, I think, and spruce, poplar, birch. Scruffy. The land is broken, rough, relatively flat. The highway arcs away from Lake Superior here. Muskeg; swamp and beaver ponds, sandy soil split open by the highway. For a time at least the huge coastal hills are gone.

Something else about roadside graffiti. Never have I seen anyone doing it.

[35]

Maybe Bellrock is like scrawling the family tree on a rock in Day-Glo paint. Inseparable from the ephemerality, though, is the defiance of the act, defiance of time, transience, mutability. Writing on a rock face doesn't lay claim to eternity, or to the rock — but to the now, to the present, to presence. It's a proclamation: the hell with my own passing, I was here! I *am* here.

What I'm doing now, driving away to work, is contained within the parentheses of Bellrock. I don't know what's more real to me, here or there.

Sign alerting tourists to Indian Pictographs.

My tape recorder sits beside me on the passenger seat. The road noise thrums inside my head.

I should be working on fiction. That's what the plan was. I just finished seven years on literary criticism.

I've been promising myself. I've accumulated openings. Fragments. Segments. A dozen years ago I completed several plays, none satisfactory, and wrote poetry, mediocre, and started novels. Novels in verse. Novels about growing up. Novels about Indians. Chronicles. Confessions. Slices of life. Erotica. Never more than a couple of chapters.

Perhaps maturity will give me an advantage. Impatiently, I wait.

three

The sky is turbulent, the lake is burnished steel. An occasional smattering of sunlight transforms the water to turquoise, cold and translucent. Islands float here and there on the surface, squared at the edges and roughly symmetrical, like whales.

The Depot Creek is a modest river, except when the water surges from the run-off after a heavy storm or when they release the overflow from one of the dams upstream, fine-tuning the system. There's a spillway at Bellrock to keep the water at more or less a constant level, even then, preventing flooding of the island or the village. After a downpour in December the rainwater will slide in sheets across the frozen ground and, in a myriad of sluiceways, join the river, as it comes to life with tremendous power, though only a nervous pattern on the surface indicates its speed.

Above the dam the river broadens into a pond the shape of a teardrop, narrowing gradually upstream a mile or so to a narrow duct where the water tumbles under a country bridge. Swamp along the edges; clear flowing in the centre but slow, so that the slightest breeze offsets the drift and the current seems to fall back upon itself. Back from the river's edge are the standing remains of dead elms, reaching up like stretch marks against the sky; or in the more lurid light of evening, like varicose veins.

The landscape is on a different scale here, along the north shore of Lake Superior; massively intricate, redundant; its beauty overwhelms, diminishes. The concept of a meadow seems absurd against this setting. Cows grazing down to the marshy river edge, slogging through the muck to get at the fresher water or to cool themselves, salve their teats; all this seems alien in the vast reaches of geography rolling by me now.

I am driving through geography.

Where I've come from, the landscape is human-proportioned. Perhaps, though, that's only from my experience of it. If I had lived here, maybe this too would seem more an extension of my own experience — or, rather, I, an extension of it. That's what I ultimately want of Bellrock, to be an extension of the landscape we live within, to participate.

Sign for Red Rock. An old friend of mine, Bill Cockburn, worked here in the early sixties. A trainee in pulp and paper. We were friends in Grade 13 at Preston High, and then through the University of Western Ontario. Close friends, during those emotionally violent years. A residual friendship kept us in touch for a long time. . . .

God how urgently we compared notes back then on our progress through the nights and days, over endless draughts of beer. . . .

Beer and lust and the intensity —

Intensity; sharing. Gone now, with growing up.

[38]

Another close friend, Jack Morgan, when I see him on rare occasions, it's as if no time has passed, at first. But the elasticity of old friendship is gone. Only the affection remains.

Memories and change.

I don't change wilfully but I've no desire to live "coherently," in a continuum, cause and effect in an endless forward gyre.

A predictable future frightens me as much as no future at all; makes living irrelevant.

1967 and 1957 and 1977 are distinct from each other, immediate and palpable in my mind . . . although the process of differentiation becomes harder as I grow older; more painful, and more necessary.

Just passed the thousand-mile mark.

Taking Jim's prophecy literally, fifty-fifty suggests the odds of a breakdown will increase as the trip progresses.

I don't push it.

Went through Thunder Bay a while back, around it actually.

On the by-pass.

Thunder Bay. Assertive. Not blunt like Penetang. Or insipid, like Penetanguishene.

Thunder Bay. Thunderbay. thunderbay

Kakabeka.

Fifteen miles up from Thunder Bay, Kakabeka Falls. Has the same effect as tintinabulation. As antedeluvian. Kakabeka Falls.

Words alive on their own. Separate (verb and noun) from meaning.

Four years ago, when Ginny and I drove through from the West, we stopped for a while at Kakabeka Falls before driving on past Thunder Bay, looking for a vacant motel or camping grounds. . . .

Nothing to focus on now. The landscape is eerily monotonous.

As if to compensate, two comical swatches of blue show through the low cloud covering — paradoxically, the blue makes the cloud more ominous.

Passing a sign that says: Arctic Watershed From Here All Streams Flow North Into The Arctic.

The clouds are low, stoop-shouldered; the blue epaulets are gone.

Outside Thunder Bay, a small Ukrainian cemetery, dotted with sky-blue Coptic crosses.

Amazing how many of these small towns, skewered by the Trans-Canada highway, are flanked by cemeteries, some of intriguing grandeur; the granite and marble stones a taunt, defiance, beside the flimsy buildings with their sagging false fronts, chipped tin signs, tawdry walls. . . .

Just crossed the Fire Steel River, a hundred miles east of Dryden. Crossed the Dead Horse River a while back. River is pretentious, an alien word; Depot Creek is closer to being a river. Fire Steel, Dead Horse, Depot! The Grand, the Speed are rivers. Sometimes the Depot Creek spreads to fifty, sixty feet and narrows in places to no more than fifteen, where it becomes suddenly rapid and deep, and then spreads and slows again almost to a stillness.

Depot, on some of the older maps, reads Deep Eau, a curious mixture of English and French that goes well with older versions of the village name, Belle Rock and Bell Roche. There were French there, working the wilderness, before the first English settlers took up land grants after we beat the Americans in 1812-14.

Here; now; nothing but miles and miles; little to see beyond more and more of little to see.

Dark is closing around.

It would be dark now, in Bellrock. I think more and more of Ginny, there, alone.

I haven't crossed a time zone yet, been going north, mostly. Northwest. It would be dark there now, for sure. The island, isolated in the darkness, comforting or lonely depending on your mood, your need. Julie and Laurie — I miss them. . . .

Love I guess is infinitely elastic. I love Ginny and I love Julie and I love Laurie. Each in an absolute way, each wholly, with my whole being. But if there were ten kids instead of two, love wouldn't divide in tenths any more than it now divides in halves — or thirds. It could be no greater in total than what I feel now. How could it be? Yet my love for each would never be less. . . .

Car far ahead, two elusive dots of red defining the contour of the road; occasional flashing fragments as its headlights illumine random slabs of landscape in the dark . . .

Now and then, beams of light, oncoming, separate suddenly and slip by in a blinding rush. I follow each residual glow in the mirror until, in a moment of inattention, it disappears . . .

Laurie insists, when she remembers, on being called Laura.

● ● ●

It's morning. Kenora. Slept well and I'm on the road again. The rain still falls, in a fine mist now, rather than the scattered blobs that smeared the windshield late last night.

Cottages and boathouses as I drive past the town, almost the same as around Port Carling a thousand miles to the southeast. I'm moving but not really getting anywhere at all.

[41]

Covered almost eight hundred miles yesterday.

For the last few hours, driving in the darkness, I played radio roulette, trying to catch and hold whatever station I could dial up, for as long as possible (or until my interest faded). Chicago or Wheeling West Virginia. I listened longest to a station from Nebraska, I didn't get the name, but the Mayor was on, talking with what seemed to me a reckless candour: Fred whatever is slow on the job, but by moving Bob whatever over him, to supervise, they might get more out of Fred and involve Bob more in his own work at the same time. Bob is a nice guy but he takes long lunch breaks . . . the city owes him a lot . . . but. Or will. When Harry whatever, in Public Works, was asked where his inspectors were . . . no answer . . . will need to be reconsidered. Harry.

It was a private conversation, no, a diatribe, beamed across the wilderness, throughout the continent, to be picked up by people like me, anywhere, in the privacy of our cars, bedrooms, on our boats in the middle of Lake Superior, all the lonely people.

The Mayor faded out. Other voices. I listened to the name Jesus stretched out and lubricated, made obscene. Profane.

Why do the true believers, when they talk religion, change their voices, take on that unctuous drawl, funereal twang, sighing resonance? Geeeezzuhs. Geeeeeeeeezzzzuhs Gahwd Awlmyteee.

Glory!

Can you tell what a person does or is, by the way he or she speaks? Not by the accent or vocabulary but by the way the mouth shapes words? The other day I heard a male figure skater interviewed and I thought, my God, he sounds exactly like Toller Cranston; speaking nasally and from the front of his face, with meticulous, even exquisite, precision; a certain mellifluous lilt suggesting the perfect gesture on ice, in full sequined regalia. Mouths shape words. No, words shape the mouth.

Is it driving or being alone that makes me so attend the sound of words. I mouth my thoughts, pin fleeting images with sounds against the car's interior.

It is the sounds I love right now, and listen for. Apart from meaning.

[42]

Just crossed into Manitoba.

Can't help but marvel at the vastness of Ontario. Stretching from 150 miles the other side of Bellrock — to here, north-west 1500 miles away. Larger than most countries.

Ginny's voice makes me think of adolescent dreams of women, remembered briefly on waking, urging a return to sleep.

It's quite pleasant driving in the rain in the daytime. The landscape around me is scruffy, flattened almost completely, the road a causeway furrowed through a rough green sea.

Must be moving off the Canadian Shield now because there's a distinct southern feeling — strange — my references are north and south although my primary direction is westward. The landscape is flat. I'm moving out of bush country quite suddenly into farmland, emerging. More and more deciduous trees, open spaces; the highway splits now into four lanes. In no more than twenty minutes I've moved from North to South — in Canadian terms.

Open road now. Horizons.

It occurred to me as I passed a small cemetery back there that Bellrock doesn't have one, for all the history of the place.

The implications are fascinating. Did people go away to die, or just to be buried? Over to Verona? Down to Harrowsmith? Did people never feel at home enough in Bellrock to stay there permanently? Was ground not consecrated around the church?

Cemeteries mark the transition from pioneer to established community. More so than the dedication of streets and the building of communal buildings. Where flesh and the earth merge, we are no longer passing through.

Cemeteries haunt the imagination far out of proportion to our actual experience of them. They keep cropping up in movies and novels, particularly in macabre opening sequences — a convenient point of departure, leading in numberless directions.

[43]

Leading back to the beginning.

A cemetery is a personal artifact. You don't go there to stand earth-high over a configuration of bones. By a grave, you commune with your own past, think of people who have touched your life. Think of living.

Inevitably people move, die, forget who's buried where, what the connections are. Cemeteries are de-consecrated, dug up, stone remnants mislaid or set in concrete in a wall around a park.

Two types of ancestry, I suppose, work in us all. Heritage and genetics. Ancestry of consciousness, heritage, most fascinates me now. Memory, history, myth hold me rapt; whereas psycho-biological generalizations and speculations seem ephemeral, austere.

A few minutes ago I flipped on the radio and picked up Winnipeg news. Voyager II was launched several days ago, on a ten-year flight and more, past Jupiter, Pluto, and God knows where. With messages about our species for alien beings. Amazing how much we take for granted! I hardly paid attention.

My grandmother would have been 110 this year. What would she think? When I lived with her in '57 for a year, when she was ninety, she took Sputnik in her stride. She'd already lived through the coming of the telephone, radio, television, and how much else. When she was born, in the small Scotch town of Granton, Ontario, near London, the world was a different place.

In my lifetime there seem to have been refinements but no radical changes in communications and transportation: discoveries now are sophisticated, beyond the layman's understanding for the most part, achieved by a trained elite, achievements that leave the rest of us in wonder. We have belief, but we have no theology.

I remember Grammy, ancient even when I was small, sitting in her chair with the broad maple arms, in her Queen Street house in Preston. She'd rock against the chair and tell stories of her girlhood in

Granton. Not really stories. Memories. Sleigh bells. Going to church by sleigh. Overturning in a snowbank. Still getting to the church on time, glowing, she'd say, just glowing from the cold. Her eyes would light up with the words. It was all still there, within her — even as a child I knew this. I was part of what she remembered, and sad that those times would never come around again. She had lived them, and I hadn't.

She'd tell of driving a horse and buggy to Lucan where her sister Jess worked in a store. In Lucan, everyone was Irish, as everyone was Scotch (not Scottish) in Granton. She'd recount how old Doc. Lang was stopped once along the Biddulph Line by some of the notorious Black Donnellys, and treated kindly. That seemed more important to her than the memory of seeing them herself when she was no more than ten or twelve and the Donnellys still several years away from death by the vigilantes in '81.

You could see the horizon some nights over towards Lucan red with fire, and everyone in Granton would know the Donnellys were burning barns again. Grammy's father, Hugh Cameron, sometimes did black-smith and carriage work for them when they had the stage line. One morning, she said, her father went out early and came back while the family was eating, and declared the trial of the Donnellys that was sup-posed to be held that day in Granton had been cancelled, the Donnellys were dead. "They've all been murdered," he told them. "All but Willie." And then, into the silence, he added the single word "Irish."

"Irish," he'd say, whenever the Donnellys came up. As if that explained everything.

Grammy's father died when the doctor pierced an abscess and irrep-arably erred. Her father was strong from his smithing, but he died three days later. Not before assuring Doc. Lang there was no ill will between them, not on his part, anyway.

One of Grammy's brothers, her only brother I think, went west well before the turn of the century. Her sisters married or stayed at home. All of them lived well into their nineties. Grammy's sister Kate lived to 104 and Grammy, born in the year of Confederation, lived to celebrate the country's Centennial and to enjoy her own.

That must have been a house to live in. All her sisters were strong and handsome, even in old age, and loved as an aggressive act. I get confused whether it was Nell or Jessie who worked in Lucan. I remember them both, later, as old women; the family house, the stove, the pump, the shaded yard.

[45]

Grammy is worked into the fabric of this country. She's part of my experience that I take within me far from the cemetery where she's buried in Preston, far from Granton where the old Cameron house is now a hairdresser's shop covered over with asphalt siding, and the yard is bare and the old pump gone.

Grammy is a part of Bellrock, too. My kids know only a little of her — she died when Julie was one, a full century between them. But in their relationship to their own time and place, she endures. Their Bellrock is a continuation of her growing up in Southwestern Ontario, of her father's Ontario and Scotland and her mother's, of her husband's Preston and of his parents' Germany early last century, and of England, my father's father's family in England and his mother's family in England, generations earlier, and her Mennonite forebearers who founded Preston, built Waterloo County, and of their ancestors, wandering Gentiles dispossessed by their ideals. In Julie and Laurie are my father's father's adventures in colonial Canada, after leaving Croyden, England, and in New Zealand sheepfarming, and in South Africa fighting a bad war, and in Canada again, a gentleman manufacturer, a young widower, his wife Errington, my other grandmother, dying after childbirth in 1911, little more than a bride.

We have to speak of this: the remembering blood needs words and images to run its course.

And Ginny's family in this country . . .

Ginny's mother's family on the west bank of the Humber, west of Toronto. Her grandmother and mother, she and Julie, were all born within a mile of one another. Her great grandparents were the first whites married in North Bay. Her grandfather might have worked with mine, my father's father Austin, in the bush around Temagami, before one settled near the Humber, to prosper as a market gardener, the other in Preston, where his brother was already prospering.

And Ginny's father's grandfather, an Irish Catholic come to the United States, a railroad accident where he lost an arm and his faith, the priest not getting there to give the last rites and him in a profound rage surviving and with a vengeance turning Methodist. No loss of faith, for its vigour multiplied. He brought up his children strict Methodists in Canada, east of Toronto, and his son was as strict with his sons and they maintained the faith until their father died and the force of their grandfather's conversion dissipated.

These; and countless others.

[46]

All, a part of the history of Bellrock, of a place and places they had never been.

It is essential in Canada to locate oneself with the land. Beyond memory there is nothing.

We have no common ancestry either genetically or in imagination. We are no longer British or French. The past of Britain and France, or of our other homelands, is no longer ours. We must re-invent the past from memory, make it our own.

Geography alone is our common ancestor.

That's why there's so much interest in aboriginal peoples in this country, responsibilities picked up for past grievances, old ways restored for their own sakes — they and the land are inseparable, their story becomes ours, what we have done to them we have done to ourselves: for them the land is kin, for us they personify the earth, our past.

Place. Bellrock.

While I drive now over indescribably flat black earth, trees clumped around farmhouses, two short hours from bushland wilderness, I think how I belong to this whole land; but uneasily. I make my way across it on a tether from the particular spot where we have established ourselves for this, our overlapping generation.

There is no horizon here, barely a limit to vision, to what I can see; another illusion.

Just passed a sign noting this is the longitudinal centre of Canada. Before or after Newfoundland joined Confederation? That surely threw the centre off.

Another sign: "Landmark." Ambiguous; what does it refer to? Itself, perhaps.

Such flatness insists that land and sky are two planes pressed against each other; a claustrophobic feeling, space and no dimension.

Haven't decided whether to stop for a bit in Winnipeg or barrel on through. I'm into the rhythm of driving.

Wouldn't mind seeing Enright, though. Or I might call Dave Arnason.

Winnipeg, a prairie city, looming. From the outskirts you can see the

[47]

central core pushed up into the sky. You can take it in, whole, until you get too close.

● ● ●

The unusual pay toll of 15¢ at the phone booth, where I stopped to make a couple of calls, made me realize how far I was from home.

Couldn't reach Bob Enright, but I met Dave at a McDonalds, the most readily recognizable landmark around. Went back with Dave and Jenny to their place for a coffee. Dave and I worked into the conversation as many lines about our current achievements as propriety allowed. Enthusiasm played through both our voices just enough to show that what we were saying was important to us, but that we didn't take ourselves too seriously. A conversation you'd expect from two people whose careers run parallel, in the same field; who since we first met at graduate school in Fredericton have chosen different options, leading in much the same direction.

Sorry I couldn't reach Enright. I tried. He's a man of excessive vitality — he must surely on his own suffer dark times because in company he is obstreperously good humoured.

Met him this spring in Nova Scotia, at a writers' conference in Halifax. We were both there as "resource" people. He and I went out to dinner with another editor, our first night there. At random we picked one of the restaurants the taxi-driver suggested. During the dinner Enright left the table and went downstairs to the washroom. He returned, strained and pale. Set both hands palms-flat on the linen cloth, and slowly shook his head from side to side. Since it was difficult eating dinner with this going on, the other guy and I sat back and waited. The lobster was getting cold. Finally he explained: "I just saw my wife. She works here." And he started to laugh.

He was from Manitoba, had never been to Halifax before. They had been divorced a couple of years back and had lost track of each other. She was working as a hostess in the downstairs lounge.

[48]

"My God," he said, "I still love her."

Our waitress came over and commented on his knowing the hostess — she had seen them talking. For some inexplicable reason, somehow misplaced gallantry, he said, "Yes, yes, that's my sister."

"Oh really! She's very nice."

"Yes," said Enright, "I know." And then, to compound the absurdity: "I used to know her very well."

The waitress smiled without flinching, and walked away with his unfinished plate of lobster.

The highest thing around me now, the hydro towers. The land is a sheer horizontal plane. Trees are smudges. Farmhouses, knots in the greying weather. Everything is distant, and I, somehow, in the dead centre, a theoretic point.

Clearly people here need stories to live within. More than elsewhere; to give their lives dimension. Words, to remember by.

Sign: prepare for eternity/you will soon be there forever.

The soil is black.

There is no structure to this land, no shape.

four

"It's me, Oh Lord, standing in the need of prayer."

It's Labour Day, a holiday. The stores are closed, so I borrowed an old tape from Dave to carry me through. There are party voices on it; singing and talk, many voices at once, having a good time.

A rousing spiritual, voices only.

My voice erases theirs. I play back and hear a snippet of song, then my voice alone. "It's Labour Day," it says. "A holiday."

The farmer we bought the house from, for the price of kindling, had taken a chain saw to the original family home and cut an opening in the back big enough to turn it into a drive shed, and used it that way until the floor collapsed. The roof and then the ceiling caved in a few years before we bought it, but the walls were still standing.

The house, now,

is a complex design;

the logs range from fifteen to twenty inches in diameter. They're cedar, except for the top and bottom logs, which are elm. The logs are partially squared but not tight fitting. The chinking between them is done in bleached cement. Outside, the logs are weathered grey. Inside, after Ginny's painful sessions with lye and a stiff brush, they're a mellow golden colour, soft and warm.

The living room runs across one side, with a stone fireplace in the end wall. A large bow window fills the gap in the back wall with a spectacular view upriver.

The other half of the ground floor, now, is taken up by the dining room and a small study, separated by stained glass windows we brought from our place in Montreal.

Upstairs, there's a sewing room, our bedroom, and a bathroom with a blue bidet, one that fountains up, not one that merely swirls. . . .

On the easterly side of the log house, behind the fireplace wall, is one of two additions, a single-storey library with leather-bound books from my grandfather Clare's collection. The shelves frame another bow window, this one looking over the water and the dock at the front. Outside, the library is sheathed in pine, rough-sawn and laid on in board and batten style, unfinished, left to weather. Cedar shingles on the roof, the same as on the log house.

There's a snug front porch on the library with gingerbread that Ginny designed and I cut out, and old pillars we bought at an auction, three for a dollar.

One whole wall inside the library is taken up by a hanging quilt that Ginny and her mother made. The rest is books and view.

The other addition is equally as integrated, through materials and design, with the log house. It is as large as the log house, but wrapped around the back corner, so to speak, so that it does not compete with the older building but complements it.

On the same level as the log house, in this part, there is a large hallway, a pantry with a freezer chest and built-in shelves, and a small laundry.

Two steps up take you into a large kitchen, with a dining-table breakfast nook, a chesterfield and, set beneath a huge old pine beam, a cooking area, with stove and grill, and a large franklin fireplace surrounded by old brick, newly placed. There's an island with a sink in the centre of the room, made of laminated maple: at one time it was a segment of a bowling alley; we picked it up from a demolition job in Montreal a couple of years ago. A compactor is tucked under the island. Six weeks of bottles and cans and plastic containers for four people can be compacted into one neat package, which I use for land fill. Papers, we burn. Bio-degradables, we put on the compost pile, for the garden.

The other bathroom is on this level, done completely in cedar. The walls are diagonal cedar boards, smooth but unfinished. The ceiling is rough cedar, reverse board and batten, also unfinished. The feel of this room is mildly soporific. The sauna is off this room, all cedar as well. Warm wood smells in winter fill your mind: with the sauna up to over 200 degrees, the only thing comparable for their dream-intensity might be freshly ground coffee or the sweet fresh smell from a newly-opened tobacco pouch, or new-mown hay in late June, still lying on the ground to dry, before it's baled.

There is also a shower, a necessary adjunct to the sauna, although even on the coldest days we sometimes roll in the snow and, when the water is open, we swim.

Doing the woodwork in this room is the closest I've come to fine carpentry. Angles upon angles. Slow and demanding and immensely frustrating; satisfying not so much for any particular detail but for the over-all effect. The vanity cabinet is cedar, as well. Cabinet-work!

Downstairs, below all this: a pump room, a small shop, a wine cellar and the kids' area, which at present is one large room, although we could in future divide it in half, if they went. Julie and Laurie are outraged when people call this room the basement, and in fact it is sunk only about three and a half feet, so the windows are above ground level.

In the corner of their room is a large rock sloping upwards into the walls. The log house sits on bedrock which drops off under the addition. When we dug out the foundation, working by hand since no machinery can get over, I tested in several spots for depth. No problem until we were almost dug out, then I discovered bedrock humped back up across the one corner. So; when we poured the footings and built the cement walls up to ground level we simply incorporated the rock into the design of their room and they now have a unique rock-garden.

To refute the hint of basement, we put a double layer of padding under their carpet, creating, inadvertantly, a trampoline effect.

Shortly after laying their carpet last spring we had the first heavy

[53]

rainstorm of the season. We were all off at a school concert, and when we came home we found four inches of water in the basement — definitely a "basement" then. The sump pump which I had installed for precisely such problems had frozen up somewhere along the drainage line during the winter. It sounded operational, but it simply swirled the water around in one spot; the waters rose and we were inundated.

It was a test of strength and sanity to hoist a soggy sopping carpet, newly laid wall to wall over a double layer of absorbent foam, all high enough after the sump pump had been restored and used to drain the flood, to get 2 by 4's underneath and aim fans and heaters under, to dry everything out with minimal smell or damage.

The kids moved up with us for a week, then back down, declaring the area no longer a basement.

Except for the foundation, Ginny has generally done the cement work, and the plastering and painting. I do the carpentry. Design we do together, as we go along. There has never been a blueprint or a master plan, even in our minds. We argue our way through to something that we both like, and want. An over-all design takes shape from the inside out.

This larger addition eccentrically works its way close around the huge sugar maple. There are smaller maples on the island, a few sugar and some soft maples, red and mountain, but only this one is of any size. When we raised the log house we had no idea the back addition would be going on. The house seemed to rise up comfortably under the lee of the tree which, apart from anything else, provided secure moorings for block and tackle in its overhanging branches to help us raise the back wall and sections of the roof. Now, it almost occupies a special room as the house jogs cosily around its base and its branches spread above, over the whole of the addition.

There's water close by on three sides of the house. Since the island is only two acres altogether, there's water all around, but from the ground floor you can't see it through the trees to the west, not in the summer, although the rays of the setting sun even then light up the island some evenings with the soft pervasive glow of a dying fire. . . .

Just passed an accident. Red and orange flashing. Sometimes I almost forget I'm driving. I could see it coming from miles away.

Police and ambulance. Small kids in one of the cars; looked okay. Gasoline and shattered glass on the road.

[54]

Julie Laurie

Time, passing.

I guess every parent has on the periphery of every conscious moment an awareness of the terrible possibilities . . . the fact of their children's vulnerability.

Sometimes while I've been driving during the last three days I've thought of myself in an accident. Listening to the radio reports as they give the death tally for the Labour Day weekend, I drive for miles with sordid images insistent on my mind. Images not of pain but of sorrow.

Statistics; inexorable. This is the holiday weekend still. I'm on the road. The car's not running properly. The tires are worn. I drive carefully. If I dwell on the statistical improbability, far from being reassured, I'm overwhelmed at the possibility, that there is in actual fact a possibility.

Every time a bus passes me and the Volvo shivers, shudders, every time I take a sharp turn and feel pressure against the tire walls, my heart races and my stomach churns, blood surges to my head and my feet absurdly tingle.

I think of that last moment of consciousness before the end, a grim fantasy I play over and over in my mind — if only I could have enough time to say goodbye, to flip on the tape recorder and say goodbye to Ginny and Julie and Laurie, just a few words refined by anguish to say exactly what I mean.

[55]

I think there can be no such thing as instantaneous death. Consciousness works beyond the pace of clock time. That blood rushing to my head; the event seems slowed almost to a series of still frames until the danger passes. There would be time to review my whole life between impact and the shattering of flesh.

Even struck from behind, a shot, a direct blow — there is still that fractional moment of awareness as the bullet penetrates, the skull collapses, time before death, until time ends.

My kids' fragility . . . there is no talk of death that does not include them in my mind, how fragile they are, a shadow to my other thoughts. There is no thing I fear that can compare.

Look into your child's eyes. You see yourself but not in reflection or duplication or vicarious alternative; look carefully, you see yourself in a genetic flow; descend there into the origin of your species; thousands upon thousands of survivors who have preceded you, made you, now take this tiny step ahead. It is all there in the link between you, the secret you hold in common.

My love for Julie and for Laurie acknowledges perpetual loss as they grow and change. The joy of love I have for them at any moment is already lost as the moment passes. Childhood time is linear change, maturity is time as spacial form; eventually our lives cannot contain us, we grow senile, and burst. Death then is appropriate, but the million deaths that come with every change as the child grows are appropriate too, each one a new beginning.

To say, child I love you, is to say, I cannot keep you. I love your changing, I love the ways you grow away from me, take possession of yourself, I love the rebellion in you that continues, between you and me, the struggle of our species, with grace, free-will, and determination to endure.

I hope my children grow away from me as shoots from a plant that work into their own space, sink roots of their own that, when mine atrophy, still grow —

I seem to be seeking the safety of metaphor.

It's hard to talk about things so close. Hard to find words that don't distort.

[56]

Just passed a huge rambling red brick house, dilapidated, verandah somewhat askew, ornate gingerbread, crumbling in places, the bricks in careful patterns here and there, gables, trees planted symmetrically around the yard. Aspirations to found a dynasty. The outbuildings have collapsed. Car wrecks litter the lawn. A painted tractor tire lying on its side sprouts plastic flowers.

Laurie is the more vulnerable. It's not that she's any less capable or resilient. If anything her feet are more firmly on the ground than Julie's. And it's not that she's younger.

I think it all stems from the different way I understand Laurie. There are vast areas of her personality I don't quite fathom, don't see, yet know are there. While seeming to be more open, I think she's intuitively more guarded than Julie, keeps much bottled up inside, revealed only indirectly.

Julie and I — too often, I find myself being hard on Julie. And then regret it. And when I indicate to her that I'm aware I've been too hard on her there's a coming together, an understanding is re-established between us. There's a continuity to our relationship. Oscillating, positive and negative continuity. With Laurie, there's more a series of intense encounters, accumulating as our relationship grows.

I'm sure, too, I inevitably worry about Laurie because of the past, long before she remembers. Ginny had a hard time carrying her. She was confined much of her term to a hospital bed, for fear of hemorrhaging to death. Laurie's twin died early in the pregnancy.

There was a very good chance that Laura wouldn't make it.

Neither Ginny nor I lose the feeling that Laurie might never have been. She carries with her as a memento of her troubled beginnings a crooked little finger, as dear to me as anything.

The land past Brandon has a slight gentle roll to it. Fields and fields, thousands of acres, of sunflowers.

• • •

Dialled up a football game on the radio. Half-time discussion. Why do sportscasters and colour-commentators always sound like caricatures of themselves? "Well, Chet." "Yes, Fred."

I used to play football in high school. Messed up my left knee. Played hockey, too, in public school. Played most sports, though not a star in any of them. But for the life of me I can't appreciate the rituals of professional team sport. The pleasures of watching other people play are beyond me.

Now going through Virden, "the oil capital of Manitoba." I had no idea Manitoba had oil.

Rather strange to drive right through the middle of town and see all these pumps, bobbing like plastic dunking birds in novelty shops. They're in farmers' fields and in town, in people's yards. Oddly, though, the houses near the pumps don't look especially prosperous. Perhaps it's a misconception that oil automatically means wealth.

The football game still mumbles like static.

Perhaps I've come up somewhat of a loner. I prefer to watch an individual competing against a standard set by himself or herself.

Ginny and I have that in common, being loners, although she can chat quite casually and comfortably with almost anyone under almost any circumstances, while I usually feel awkwardly constrained and often only summon up a modicum of conversation through fear of being thought discourteous. Or stupid. Or empty.

She makes friends more readily, but only part of her personality is given over to any but the most intimate relationship. Different people who feel they know her well may know quite different people in fact.

I remain guarded, but in other ways. I suspect my personality so hopelessly lacks integration, coherence, that I couldn't possibly present separate aspects of it convincingly. Obliquely, and in fragments, I present it all at once. This leads people to feel they don't know me very well, no matter how much they actually do.

Ginny's personality is somewhat like the many-faceted surface of a diamond. I come across more like the light fragments on a disturbed pool of water, where there is nothing constant but the whole of it.

Sometimes I think our marriage consists in the inevitability of our being together: two very separate people, alone, who need and touch and use and sometimes hurt each other. We've had some rough times. Bellrock is as much a product of working those times through as of common aspirations. We quarrel more than we should, and we're

[58]

capable of hurting each other, and do, although always we hold something back. There are things we know about each other, things that might be said and done that would be devastating, beyond forgiveness. We have never been that desperate. We have been vulnerable to each other, as the best of lovers are, and, no matter how upset, neither of us has violated that trust. We do not hold back in an argument in order to keep something in reserve, but because even at our worst we both realize, somewhere deep within, that the storm will pass and we will have to live with what has been said and done.

I just crossed over into Saskatchewan.

We never hesitate to have our arguments in front of the kids. I'm sure many would see that as a terrible thing. But the kids know we fight and they also know we work our way through these times and make up and they know we share many great experiences together, many of which they can only understand in part, and they know, at the ages they're at, that sometimes these are sexual and sometimes in solemn private friendship and sometimes almost spiritual, and they know that sometimes they are included in what Ginny and I are together and sometimes they are not.

The kids know we spend a lot of good time together, talking and not talking; working together, hammering our way towards some conclusion or another. How to build something, how to paint something, where to put something — Bellrock has shown them a great deal more of us than we could have anticipated, and I think that it is a good thing, for all of us.

Ginny and I are best friends.

But more. There is an open show of affection that friends often can't afford to show — there is a reserve to friendship that doesn't exist between us as lovers, that makes us more volatile, and more vulnerable, but there is also a commitment at even the meanest domestic level that lovers seldom share.

We are partners, and we shape each other's lives.

Just passed a cemetery without markers; a single sign, Memorial Garden. Not a very exciting place.

I think Ginny will be around to bury me. Or, less likely, given the actuarial odds, I'll bury her. It's a good thing we have, together.

Ginny is a very determined person, able to direct herself, her behaviour, and shape her experience, by application of inner resources, intelligence, imagination. She certainly is not easy to live

[59]

with — although I suspect she is easier than I am. Objective judgement is impossible, but that seems to be the prevailing opinion between the two of us.

We are interesting to each other.

Ginny spent the summers when she was a kid on an island near Honey Harbour, on Georgian Bay. Our mutual affinity for islands was not come by arbitrarily, although we didn't set out to merge and manifest our childhood memories, either.

I was offered a job here once, at the University of Saskatchewan in Saskatoon. I wonder if I had taken it, would Bellrock have been as necessary? Or more so?

I feel a certain empathy with this province. I know that's absurd: I'm driving through and should be out the other side either tonight or in the morning. But I feel a closeness, sort of the way I did for New Brunswick. And do for Southeastern Ontario.

The beauty here is rugged, but not majestic or sublime as in the great mountain ranges of British Columbia, or along the Atlantic coast, or in the Arctic, as I imagine it, though I've never been there, all the way.

Here there is a tenuous harmony worked out between the people and the land they're living on, the environment they're living in. Evidence of a productive truce: the grain elevators I'm passing by; the comfortable farmhouses scattered on the gently rolling land. Man seems a peaceful but temporary occupant, his marks erasable in a few short years, as they are around Bellrock where so many of the old farms have fallen through disuse to their primal state, the buildings crumbled, old fence-lines shown only by the symmetrical lay of trees across fields too brulie now even to be much good for pasture. "Brulie" is a local word, I imagine from the early French, to describe land so rough and scruffy it has no practical use at all.

I feel at home here, too, from infant memory. During the War we lived in Saskatoon for a year, while Dad taught navigation at the Air

Force Base, back from active duty overseas with an ear problem; he left from Halifax, told Mom in private code, I think I'll drop in to see Aunt Millie tomorrow, which meant he was on his way to England. A year later he was back and we moved around with him — Victoriaville Quebec, Saskatoon, Rivers Manitoba, from Blair to Preston, to his father's house — I guess it wasn't that much moving after all, but memories of my first five years seem dominated by images of motion, and of alien places, externals. In Saskatoon I remember chasing pigs at the Agricultural College with the promise I could keep my catch. I remember Aunt Beth coming to visit, seeing her there. I remember a particular car-ride, but I don't remember why I remember it. And sleeping in a hotel. And a train, the station, Richard being frightened, no, me; and a washroom on the train, other mysteries, the joy of motion. I remember seeing, countless acts of seeing.

Visual memories. A flutter of images; labyrinth of words.

There's a hypnotic effect to this highway and this land. Lines that define nothing; planes. At times I'm disoriented. Have I missed Regina? Did I stop for dinner yet? Prairie can be discombobulating — a lovely silly word. Like tintinabulation. These are words you seldom say, except self-consciously, mouthing them. There are others that I can't say at all. Not forbidden words, but defiant. I-n-c-h-o-a-t-e — I spell it but the syllables escape me. Or, try to wrap my mouth around, again I spell it, c-h-t-h-o-n-i-c. I should look these up and practise them. But why? I can always say tintinabulation, discombobulation, cellar door, rococco, Kakabeka Falls, Shubenacadie. And wilderness.

Bellrock is an island.
The early days of our marriage weren't devoted to searching for an island refuge. Bellrock just happened to us.

In the autumn of 1968 Ginny's mother, Enid, went to an auction north of Kingston to buy a small refrigerator she had seen advertised. Three years earlier, after Ginny's father had died (and a few months before we were married), her mother had taken over management of the family business, the Royal Hotel in Kingston — which once, under a different name, belonged to Sir John A. Macdonald's intimate friend, Mrs. Grimason. The dream of Canada was, if not conceived there, certainly nurtured. Anyway, Enid was in the process of converting the rooms upstairs over the tap room into apartments. The upstairs dining room, which is still intact, was the meeting place for Sir John A. and his cronies for years. Long after he became Prime Minister. He held the hotel mortgage at one point, and signed it over to Mrs. Grimason, who is now buried, alongside her husband, within spitting distance of Sir John A.'s grave, nearly as close to him as either wife.

Enid went to the auction, which turned out to be in Bellrock, to buy a fridge for one of the apartments. The house where the sale was being held was also up for auction, along with the acre of land it sits on between the mill and the dam. With the pond above and the stream and sluice converging below, it too is an island, in theory at least. The house had been a store before the turn of the century, and was used for a while as a school, according to old maps. The drive shed had been a small cheese factory, although evidence of that is rather ambiguous. The house had no water, no insulation, only a space heater; but it appeared structurally sound. Enid is not impulsive, but on the other hand she is quick to make a decision, and for a remarkably modest sum she bought the place when it was auctioned off as the final sale of the day.

Now the land is smooth and swelling. There are no hills, really, no protrusions; just great huge sweeping swells. The farms must be very rich because the fields are cultivated, almost manicured, and yet the farmhouses are few and far between.

I've driven through before, coming back from the Coast four years ago with Ginny, but with someone in the car I don't think I took in nearly as much of the world around me, even when we weren't talking.

Another cemetery just went by. It's a relief to see gravestones instead of dead cut flowers and nothing rising.

The north-east shore of Lake Superior is overpowering, but at least it's a variation of what I know, an exaggeration of what I'm used to. I've seen flat fields before, too, but I could hardly say I've therefore seen the Prairies in miniature.

It's as if someone had pulled the landscape at the corners to stretch it smooth, and trapped bubbles of air underneath which lift the surface in formless contours.

There's a curious intimacy here between the highway and the fields, stretching endlessly away; no fences. There are different coloured fields, green, golden, earth-black, grain-brown. Fences only around homes — of course — no livestock! This is growing land, not grazing.

There are no rocks here to speak of. Around Bellrock, stone outcroppings shape the fields into unimaginably intricate designs, and the land is useable only where a tractor can reach and the soil has sufficient depth, or where enough sparse grasses grow for grazing; otherwise it is overgrown with scrub alders and brush, or bush, or submerged in beaver ponds and marshes. Brulie. These fields here have disconcerting symmetry. This is a landscape of straight lines and curves, not ragged edges.

A hundred yards across the mill pond from Enid's place, and virtually indistinguishable from the far shore, is what the old maps show as Goose Island. It has a dense growth of pines, someone's reforestation project fifty years ago. I've talked to older people who played on the island as kids, when there were only a scattering of taller pines, a few oaks and maples, a couple of birch. These are mostly there still, along with remnants of elms that died from Dutch Elm disease, some alders and clumps of sumach, raspberry brambles and long grasses in the sunlit patches. The island was by virtue of its relative isolation something of a bird sanctuary, and although we've built our house there, on the southeast corner under the great sugar maple, it remains so, now. So many birds! A loud noise at night among the trees will set the air alive with beating wings.

The year after Enid bought her place, the summer of '69, when she had already begun the process of turning it into a comfortable summer home, Ginny and Julie and I lived there. Ginny was carrying Laurie, and spending a lot of time in the hospital. I was a graduate student with no great prospects. We had no income beyond what I could

[63]

scrounge through odd jobs, driving a cab, slinging beer, working as a painter's helper.

That summer we approached Don Ritchie, the farmer who owned the island, and asked what he'd take for it. We knew he had turned down other offers, but for reasons of his own he decided to let us have it, and for terms so open we felt we could manage.

The winter of '69-'70 we lived in Galt, in my Aunt Marge's house, while I completed a Master of Philosophy degree in English at the University of Waterloo. Laurie was born safely, and Julie turned three.

The academic year drew to a close and Ginny and I had both been accepted for graduate work at the University of New Brunswick in the fall. We needed a place for the summer. It was Ginny's idea to put the money that we would have spent on rent into camping equipment and build a semi-permanent camp on the island which we could use through the academic summers ahead, when we anticipated having little money and the need for a refuge to study and unwind.

I was reluctant. Nevertheless, we found a large tent on sale, which we tested in Aunt Marge's living-room, an eight by fourteen foot blue and orange extravaganza among her fine antiques. Later we bought a smaller tent, a propane stove, a chemical toilet, odds and ends like axes, hammer, saw, and nails.

In early May I started the first building project I had ever under-taken. In Grade Nine I was passed through a manual training course out of kindness, not for any demonstrated competence. I knew how to wield an axe from working in the bush around Temagami in my teens as a canoe trip guide, although all I'd ever cut were firewood and tent poles.

At the end of a month we had a substantial tent platform, twenty feet square, built from logs cut on the island and topped with plywood, with both tents set up on it, along with a picnic table and a kitchen area — a cottage with no walls. In the large tent we placed our bed, an antique dresser Ginny had refinished, a small table, two chairs, a bookcase, a few plants, all the comforts of a summer home. In the other tent the kids had a small bed they shared and a dresser; we had a crib in there as well, the first summer. Near the platform was a small shed, one half separated for the chemical toilet and the other used for storage.

That same month I also built a dock, making a crib from our own logs and filling it with stones dredged from the river bottom, running

[64]

Remains of original 1840 log house near Croyden, Ontario, 1968.

Summer living beside the building site.

Preparing the base for rebuilding at Bellrock, 1969.

Setting the top log in place.

Winter, 1971.

Log house nearly complete; tent platform being dismantled, 1971.

Downstream; the mill and village across the pond.

Front door.   *Library porch.*

Living room

Living room.

Quilt by Ginny and Enid.

Julie and Laurie, 1977.

Laurie and weanling Morgan, 1978.

Laurie and Julie, Halloween, 1978.

Laurie, John, Julie and Paddy, 1977.

Julie on her sixteenth birthday, 1982.

Kitchen at dusk.

Julie, Ginny and Laurie, 1983.

Ginny, 1980.

John, 1980.

logs out to the crib from shore, and covering the whole thing with old cedar planks hauled down from Muskoka, where they had been thrown out when the boathouse was repaired the previous spring.

For the next five years this was where we spent our summer months, from May through to September.

Crude as it was, the dock was substantial. We replaced it in the spring of '76 with a new dock, closer to the house and farther away from the village, where we have more privacy and deeper water for swimming. We had a time dismantling the old one. And the abandoned tent platform, while spongy here and there on top, had to be hacked apart with an axe, it was so ponderously solid. Lilies grow where the old dock had been and where the platform was the grass is green and a couple of small maples we transplanted have taken root.

The following summer, 1971, home from New Brunswick, we decided to build a stone barbeque with a screened-in gazebo affair surrounding it, for toasting marshmallows without being devoured by carnivorous insects. Mosquitoes, especially. From mid-May until July 1st. The tents, filled with fly-spray, were our only refuge.

Ginny thought the pinkish gleam of feldspar granite would make an attractive barbeque. There is an abandoned feldspar mine only a mile away, three miles by road. As we brought more and more feldspar over to the Island, we came to realize that we had somehow engineered our way, through naive and grandiose conceptualizing, into a behemoth project. The rock itself insisted on becoming a fireplace; a whole eight by eight foot wall of the gazebo began to fill with feldspar, each rock meticulously placed, each with a thousand razor-edged facets, impossible to shape, cantankerous in handling.

We learned from a book how a fireplace is made, how there must be a smoke ledge so it will draw properly, how the back should slope towards the front, how the proportions of flue to hearth are crucial (although size is relative, not absolute), how the fireplace shapes the air as a sort of negative sculpture, the harmonious relation of its spaces determining whether it will work effectively or not. What we didn't read was how to work with stone, how to build the solid forms that surround the spaces. It never occurred to us that a stone fireplace might not be built of solid stone.

By the end of the summer our project outgrew the gazebo concept. It rose ten feet in the air, was eight feet wide, four feet deep, and contained 16,000 pounds of feldspar, all of which had been loaded piece by piece into our Volvo station wagon, driven to the far shore, lowered gingerly into a rowboat, rowed across the pond, unloaded, carried twenty feet to the building site, piled, sorted, selected, hoisted up, fitted, cemented. Cleaned off and given quiet blessing. Cement and sand had to be brought over, too. Bellrock had its own Stonehenge.

Both of us found it impossible to work wearing gloves. At times our fingers literally dripped blood at the end of the day when we retired to the tent; yet as our rock mound grew and took shape so did our pride and pleasure in what we were doing. It works perfectly now, spilling only the tiniest wisp of smoke at the left front corner until the chimney heats up. Even standing there alone on its rocky base it drew well.

While we worked, Julie played close by. Laurie dangled in a basket from a pine bough; or, in her Jolly Jumper, she would use the spring of the branch to keep a rolling bouncing motion going for hours on end, an indifferent witness to our labours, content with growing from six to nine months old.

In the last week of the summer, before we went back to Fredericton, we capped the fireplace with cement and went off to visit Margaret Laurence, who had agreed to serve on the Editorial Board of the *Journal of Canadian Fiction*. Its founding was another project of that same summer; as well as studying for my Comprehensive Exams. I remember explaining the tattered flesh on our fingertips, bandaged piecemeal with a plethora of band-aids, and Margaret accepting the story as perfectly natural, an odd response; in retrospect, imaginative. Driving home that evening we passed a dilapidated log house in a lilac grove near Croyden, high on a hill overlooking a lush meandering valley. The long rays of the setting sun cast a soft sheen over the abandoned ruins. Still, they looked intimidating; beyond redemption.

Before we returned to Fredericton for the winter we struck a deal to haul it away, come spring.

The log house on the hill. No roof, no windows, no doors, some of the logs lying askew; grass had grown up high around it, masses of lilacs close against it. As we approached it that evening on foot we saw that the ceiling beams had caved in, and the floors had collapsed into a rocky basement. Grass grew in earth-filled crevices in the logs. The back had a yawning gap the size of a garage door. The weatherside had rotted almost through. That was where the fireplace would go. Said Ginny.

Refuse was strewn about, cow manure caked against shards of weather ravaged wood.

From the front, the house was a cross-eyed derelict, eyes and nose formed by the T-shape of the windows hard against the front-door opening, a common characteristic of the more primitive log dwellings in the area. A mouth was formed by the rotting bottom log, upon which the upper rows pressed precariously.

I guess what I felt was dismay. Sadness, too, for what had once been someone's home.

It had been a good day. Rather than risk the minor conflagration of talking Ginny out of it, I agreed that we'd come back, try to track down the owner and at least talk to him. When you are, in your own estimation, entirely inadequate as a carpenter, no project is too absurd to be considered. You don't know enough to get out of it; but you do know enough to worry.

It could at least be used for firewood, assuming the wood was sound enough to split.

Next day we found the old man who owned it, a Mr. South who lived alone in a newer farmhouse, a century old, about a mile along the road away from Croyden. With the buffer of a winter in New Brunswick between me and reality, I went along with whatever Ginny wanted. She indicated we should make an offer. I shrugged ambiguous assent.

Mr. South was more hesitant. He seemed downcast when he realized we really wanted the place; till then he'd been quite happy to enjoy the unexpected company. "I was born there," he said. "It's old. My father was born there. Died here, though."

With a little prodding and sympathy we found it wasn't sentiment that worried him, but the financial end of things. After talking around the subject, as you do in the country, circling until seemingly of its own accord it ambles into the open, we came to common ground. He spoke slowly.

"Not a young lad," he said, referring to himself. He was in his eighties. "Got a girlfriend in Napanee." He hesitated. "It's old and it's not worth much but I'm going to ask a lot for it." He paused again. "I don't think you really want to pay that much."

He waited, weighing the silence.

"I know I wouldn't pay much for it myself, I wouldn't pay at all. What I want, now. Or maybe not." He paused, waiting, shifting on the kitchen chair. "Well maybe I'll take a hundred dollars for it and nothing less and it'll have to be in cash. I won't take a cheque."

He would have taken seventy-five. We agreed to a hundred — though we didn't agree too fast, so as not to spoil it for him.

Many were the nights — not as lyrical as that may sound — when I lay awake in Fredericton the following winter, wondering about that log shell, wondering what we were going to do with it, how we'd get it down, transport it, get the logs over to the island. Ginny would tell me not to worry, we'll manage, and roll over to sleep. I'm not sure what gets us through — her confidence or my worrying.

Ginny perhaps already envisioned the casual elegance of our present living room with its blue Liberty print curtains, which she made up from material we bought in London a couple of years ago; or conjured in her sleep the floor planks two inches thick and fifteen inches wide, magnificent slabs of wood running the full length of the house without a break; or envisioned the smoke-blue Indian rug, the old pine furniture, the plants, the books. . . . I wonder what she dreamed while I was sweating there beside her about dry rot, wet rot, engineering feats beyond comprehension. In my darker moments I suspected she had no idea at all of what we were getting into.

Spring. We returned; I think a bit to Mr. South's surprise. In a few days Ginny and I dismantled the house. With the help of her brother Michael and a friend, we loaded everything usable onto a rented truck and in several trips hauled it all to Bellrock. On the last trip we left Mr. South standing alone in the early evening beside the shambling pit where his family home had been for a hundred and forty years.

Several times after, we called in to see Mr. South, but he wasn't around. Last summer there was a For Sale sign on his house, marked "Sold."

It's probably best he can't see the place now. It has little to do with his memories anymore. Even the building shape was changed as we discarded the bottom round, shifted windows, raised the roof to an angle of our own determination and added a gable at the front. Other changes. It no longer looks cross-eyed. We separated the windows — between one of them and the door was a cupboard area shielded from the elements only by the thickness of a single board. That must have been their refrigerator years ago, during the winters. What remains are the logs themselves, but the logs, as shaped and fitted, cleaned and freshly chinked, show the work on them both of Mr. South's forebears, and of our own hands. In a strange way, his ancestors have become ours. The marks they made and we made are indistinguishable now.

I don't know how he'd have taken it.

Started into Regina but I'm turning around and heading back out to the by-pass. I'll go on to Moose Jaw for dinner.

I guess I've been pushing pretty hard, but I want to keep driving while it's daylight.

Was it only this morning I was in Kenora? Ontario? Moving through space and time with such uniform velocity, both are distorted.

It's dusk already, a slow late-summer evening, not autumn yet.

What bothers me about night driving: the visual world closes around in shadow layers of darkness; you can't see the occupants of oncoming cars, and just silhouettes occasionally in the ones ahead; you're thrust narrowly in upon yourself; you're just a pair of eyes, the feel of hands on the wheel, shapeless in the dark.

On the road fifteen hours today, so far.

That's got to be the University of Regina I'm driving by — the architecture is a dead giveaway. On the other side of the highway (I'm moving west again) is a hospital. Or a community college. In either case, intentionally formidable.

Royalty and the Church have been patrons of great architecture in the past, and today in Canada it's the universities; they've sponsored some of the finest buildings around, and some of the worst.

Didn't take long, actually, to get away from Regina. It's a tight

[69]

cluster behind me, now, sitting on top of the prairie, roots only cellar-deep.

I thought around Winnipeg that the flatness was absolute, but here the landscape is so flat there is no horizon. The land just fades away beneath surrounding walls of sky. So flat I can genuinely believe the world is round, its shoulders sloping off equally in all directions from the moving point where I am now, the moving centre. Now, and now, and now.

Like being in mid-ocean during a great calm.

I flipped the radio on, to fight sensory deprivation. All I can bring in are pop stations from Regina.

It's darker now.

There's no dimension; only textured surface in the twilight.

I'd love to share this with Julie, the dying evanescent light. Sometimes we lie together on the dock and watch the stars on a clear moonless night, when they are limitless and dazzling, and Julie never runs out of curiosity, never becomes bored with the quiet and awesome sight. She seems almost to consider it all there for her, and it would be an affront to go inside while the sky is still so full.

I worry about Julie more, as I move farther and farther away. Of the three, perhaps she needs me the most —

At the present time, anyway. My yearning to be with them, especially Julie, is shadowed by guilt, almost a sense of betrayal.

Julie's ten. She has a fine mature ability with words and a loving fascination with their sounds and rhythms and the tricks they play in the mind and on the page. She's not reckless with words, as Laurie is, who comes up with gleefully delightful malapropisms. But she has a lovely feel for words and a curiosity about them.

Julie has a tremendous integrity that can be infuriating. It makes her more honest to her inner world than to worlds imposed upon her. She's very bright, personable, does well in school. She's cute; has a

[70]

dramatic, dynamic imagination that somehow shows in her face, her posture even. It's this honesty to herself that makes me worry about her, wish that I could be there. Julie knows that I understand — not her private vision, but that she has one; not why she is separate from others, but that for her it is a necessity, sometimes painful, sometimes exquisite. I look deep into Julie's eyes and I feel comfortable there.

I look into Laurie's eyes — she insists on being called Laura these days — and in her eyes I see mystery. Their depths fascinate me, frighten me a little.

Lights of a city ahead. It's impossible to tell how far off. The earth seems to dip down between us, the dark closing in around me. Probably I'll stop soon, have dinner, settle into some late night driving, fiddle with the radio a bit. And try not to ruminate too much.

Julie wears pig-tails and will absolutely not suffer them to be cut.

I wish . . . can't even let myself articulate . . . it's pitch dark now, I wish . . . I could sneak in, kiss them without waking them, except for a sleepy hug, and then crawl in beside Ginny, sleeping, and sleep.

I remember driving through wilderness before Thunder Bay, this feeling of wanting to pull over to the side of the road and simply get out of the car and walk off into the bush, straight away from the road; simply walking. Strange, because the fantasy has no end. I think it, and then it slips away until some outcropping of wilderness invokes it again.

● ● ●

Morning. Swift Current, Sask. I was stopped short last night by the full force of a spare-rib dinner. I'd been hoping to reach Medicine Hat but it was late, past eleven when I finished eating.

Dinner was accompanied by the music of a two-man band called Too Bad. The name seemed fitting.

After a seven-hundred-mile drive, with paranoia, nurtured by so many hours alone, skimming around just beneath the surface of my mind, the audience seemed a force of occupation. At the same time, they were all at home, with me the only stranger in the room.

Halfway through the ribs, a fight erupted between a waiter and some guy who refused to be booted out and therefore was having his head pounded with a hammer fist while tucked under the waiter's arm.

The fight resumed intermittently throughout my meal, the ejected patron returning with more and different friends each time, who stood by watching him get thrashed and helping him out again, to catch his breath in the parking lot, I guess, and replace lost blood with rye. I had to slide back once as they careened against my table, which a waitress expertly steadied until they passed.

What scares me about physical fighting, getting into a fight myself, is not the pain but the humiliation of being at the centre, and out of control. I'm big, but I don't feel big. In the few fights I've been in, I've seldom known what I was fighting about — my heart was never in it; and the observer in me invariably wished, rather benignly, that I was somewhere else.

By the time I finished my meal, all I wanted to do was retreat to a quiet room and a soft bed, and to sleep. Long after I went upstairs I could hear clashing against the night the sounds of voices and bottles and squealing tires as the fight continued. Eventually, I drifted off.

[72]

five

A few splotches of blood on the ground, near where the car was parked, dried to a leathery colour.

Checking out, the woman at the desk asked me, did I sleep alright?

Catch myself speeding this morning. Bright sunshine, blue air. Breaking the 70 mark which I vowed, given the precarious condition of the engine, I wouldn't do.

As long as I keep on rolling the engine runs smoothly (the Volvo is never quiet), but when I slow down through a town or at a crossroads or when I pull in for coffee or gas, the whole car shudders towards self-destruction. There seems to be a wow in the steering although the road is good — gently undulating landscape, the thickness of the pavement almost all that lifts the car above the surface plane. Hardly a cut through the land or a built-up ridge.

The right front tire. Jim, in Verona, pointed it out before I left, giving it a kick and laughing — "Don't want to kick that one too hard, do I?"

Enough threads showing through you could put a polish on them!

I haven't worried much about the tire, more worried about the engine. A tire can be replaced.

The only time it seemed a threat was driving up from Sault Ste. Marie to Thunder Bay. Some of those curves cut pretty sharp, and dropped off sheer at the edges. I'd hate to have blown a tire there, and with the extra strain it could have happened, more likely than here, anyway; but it didn't. I did try to avoid leaning the car too heavily to the right, on the counter-clockwise curves.

I should put on the spare for sure before I hit the Rockies.

Waking up in Swift Current this morning was quite a surprise. The landscape around me had changed dramatically from what I had seen at nightfall, several hours before stopping. Much more dramatic change than after my first two nights, in Sault Ste. Marie and Kenora — perhaps because I know bush-country better and anticipate the changes there from shadows seen against the darkness.

Here, the landscape falls away from me on every side, the world a sphere and I, theoretic, moving, staying the same, seeming still. The land undulates, the horizon equidistant, the earth sloping around beneath me.

Makes me think of Waterloo County. I don't know why, it's not the same.

I picked up a young couple hitchhiking last night about a hundred miles out of Swift Current. The girl chattered pleasantly non-stop but the man said virtually nothing, grunting a few times from the back seat, smoking, feigning sleep. I kept an eye on him constantly through my rearview mirror, wary, not really sure what I expected him to do but unnerved by his silence, his indifference.

I won't take on any more hitchhikers.

They distracted me from the somewhat maudlin course my thoughts were taking. In a way that seemed more violation than relief.

Just passed a dead cow lying bloated on its side, off the road. Like a puffed bladder, four legs thrust incongruously against the air, a grisly comic thing.

I listened for a while last night to a re-broadcast of an unidentifiable old radio programme. A woman's voice at one point declared with ingratiating petulance, "I'm only a woman." And later, a voice with a quasi-Mexican accent said, without irony, "Señor, a man of your calibre should not have to speak any language except English." Golden oldies!

I switched off to darkness. Sentiment and cynicism mixed and took a morbid turn. I picked up the hitchhikers.

• • •

Driving, thinking. . .
last night in Swift Current when I couldn't sleep, the thought came to me, and kept coming back, haunting me as I lay there, that this is my novel. That I'm living it, making it from the inside out.

As soon as I admit the process, I become fiction. The world becomes a closed form.

Salt ponds alongside the road now. The landscape is nubby. I feel quite anxious this morning, I'm not sure why. I've had enough of describing landscape. This is turning into a travelogue.
It was to be about Bellrock.
That's what I've been talking about, though.

[75]

Sign for Medicine Hat. Such blatant comedy adds to the greyness of my mood.

Sign for Piepot. No, I'm closer now. Piapot. Names fascinate. Medicine Hat. Moose Jaw.

When I was a kid travelling by train, usually on my way up to Port Carling (and even very young I'd be travelling alone), I'd pass through the back yards of people's lives, small towns along the way. Towns, just names and rapid images, blurring in my mind. Some towns with no name, no word for them if the sign was missing from the station, or if I missed seeing it. Backyards. Cross-streets. I remember realizing all the lives in those places were being lived separately from mine. The thought appalled me, and appalls me still.

Just passed under a magnificent hawk perched incongruously on a hydro-line insulator. Wings folded serenely. Watching me.

It's always disconcerting to discover that worlds other than your own are real. Stop, right now. Envision a street, a small town, trees, houses set well back, people talking; one stoops, picks up a ball and throws it to a bunch of kids, walks on. In colour, in your mind, play it through. Trees, leaves, a blue sky, a pleasant day. Where was it? Was it, for a minute, real?

I distrust facts, the same as I distrust photographs.

I swam the Hellespont in September, 1962. From Abydos to Sestos; one of them now, or then, a NATO installation and the other still a town, thousands of years old. I was hung over terribly. In the *Chanakale Espres* account, the only words I recognized were my name and Lord Byron's. A romantic gesture, re-enacting facts. The picture was of Lord Byron.

What's wrong now? I don't know, I feel uneasy. Letting anxiety at leaving Bellrock turn to guilt, betrayal, leaving the kids, leaving Ginny on her own. She can cope but she'll be alone too much. The house a promise, unfinished.

This, and apprehension about what lies ahead.

In a week, I'll be teaching classes at UBC. A new place, confusing circumstances, far away. Fear, taking hold.

I don't want to be fiction.

There seems to be an impenetrable barrier between now here, and then there. There, in a classroom at the University of British Columbia. Almost as if it might not happen. And there, Bellrock, almost as if it never was.

I don't have that feeling yet, of inevitability; that suddenly I'll be in Vancouver, and all this will be retrospect.

Anticipating the completion of something unnerves me, knowing that when the anticipated future comes, then the time between will have been eliminated, not just irretrievably lost, but collapsed to nothingness.

Sometimes I think when I die there will be a brief and infinite moment when I am aware that there is nothing more, and that nothing was.

New fences, barbed wire. Scruffy bumpy grassland, congregations of tough-looking cattle. I've been through North, through Prairies, now this, unmistakably, West. Horizon continually shifts around me. I can see miles in one direction and in other ways, the folds of land loom right over the road. Minutes later they bend away, peel back, I rise upon a hill, see all ways, now dip into the land again, deep, and the horizon swings. . . .

[77]

It would be good land to ride. Julie and I could bring Lady and Troy; if it were next year and we had another horse, Laurie could be with us. Ginny would follow by bicycle, or lead the way — on our combined treks around Bellrock, she makes better time than we do over a long haul. The horses can't exaggerate their muscles through machinery. This would be good land to ride in. Not "on." The preposition is important. In Ontario, it would be "through."

To be in keeping with the locale I could switch back to riding Western. When I bought Troy last year I took a few lessons in English, and now I find it more enjoyable, working together with the horse, rather than being perched on top of it.

Just passed into Alberta.

Hadn't realized before, but about thirty miles back I passed the two-thousand-mile mark from home. Two-thirds of the way, now.

Julie rides both Western and English. When we got Lady we picked up an old intricately hand-tooled Western saddle. But this summer, Julie and Laurie took lessons, tried English, and after a month, twice a week, they were really taken with it and asked if we could get an English saddle. I think Julie feels she's betraying something — she's quite assertive about not giving up Western entirely.

Laurie is seven and a fabulous rider, with great balance from riding Lady since she was four without being able to reach the stirrups.

Julie and Laurie and I are comfortable on horses. Ginny has made several efforts, but takes no pleasure in it. She seems disturbed by the willfulness of a horse, disturbed when the horse doesn't respond to body commands with the alacrity and grace of a well-handled bicycle.

The sense of not being in full control disturbs Ginny profoundly, and of course most horses by nature seem to feel bound to press their advantage.

The kids and I fool around a lot in the paddock, going through figure-eight courses and over homemade jumps. When we go on hacks through the countryside, Laurie will ride her bike along with Ginny; she would even if we had another horse. Laurie isn't a martyr, but she's enormously generous and considerate. She'd hate for Ginny to be left out. I think part of Laurie's vulnerability is that she's so open-hearted. She always seems to question her own motives, though, terrified of being considered a goody-goody, to use Julie's expression for it.

Heard on the radio from Medicine Hat: "Mere girls are not as mere as they used to be." God I get sick of people sometimes. My girls are fighters, but victims inevitably of such stupidities.

[78]

Sometimes the stridency of Ginny's feminism gets me down; sometimes her anger seems directed at being a woman. Bitterness is an admission of defeat. But then I look at Julie and Laurie and the world around them, and I hurt; I listen to people who insist the battle's over, won with a few bits of legislation, a few barriers torn down, and I get bloody angry. I think of our society built on ideology, on theologies that fear women, despise them, and I cry that my children will be fighters, be tough, and never lose the sensitivity to know what they're fighting for and why. Never lose pride in their humanity and in being women.

I sometimes feel my daughters are players in a game where only their opponents know the rules.

Houses appear in pairs along the route every now and then: one will be a bungalow, clapboard or aluminum-sided, large double-glazed windows, boxy, suburban neat. Tucked back further from the road, the other house will be old, weathered, two-and-a-half stories with a verandah, gabled — gingerbread not as ornate as in rural Ontario — gaping black holes where the eyes have been, wood weathered silvery grey. Such old houses refuse to collapse, and perhaps their ghosts, private to the families that live in their shadow, keep back the wrecker's hand. Although the new house has replaced them, they remain alongside as a spectral presence of the past.

This same impulse to transfer lives from cantankerous farmhouse to the convenience of a suburban fragment leads most local Bellrock people to look on us with dismay, builders, paradoxically, of an old house, one far from the road at that. On an island.

Calgary's only a couple of hours away. I'll stop in for a visit with my brother Steve and his wife Carla. I phoned them last night from Swift Current to let them know I was coming. Told them I'd only stay a while, and then get farther along the road before stopping for the night, closer to the end.

[79]

I'm not looking forward to driving through the mountains. The farther I get today, the less tomorrow.

I'm not as worried about the car as I was. Statistically, chances are increasing that it's going to break down. But this is the last third of the journey. If necessary I could leave it behind and return for it on a weekend. The front right tire seems to be thumping on the tar patches.

I'm not a mountains person. Some people are lifted out of themselves by mountains; almost a transcendent experience. I like landscape where everything is human-proportioned, and yet seems to stretch off infinitely out of sight into the rest of the world.

Depot Creek soothes the shore around our island and I know eventually its water will reach Lake Ontario, the St. Lawrence, the Atlantic. It doesn't hammer away at us, though, insisting on the extravagance of its destiny. The Bellrock landscape depends on consciousness to give it shape and meaning.

Mountains are discontinuous with the world. They're insistent, garrulous, garish, great, soaring snow-topped aberrations.

I worry less about the car than about how I'll respond if something goes wrong with it. Car problems always flood me with frustration, a sense of my own inadequacy. With no control over the mechanism, I can barely cope. Tears and rage surge stupidly inside me. Hatred of the machine. Self-pity.

Like Ginny, riding a horse: mirror images of each other. The same, and opposite.

She's comfortable with machines; and people.

I'm better, I think, with animals.

Riding now on a perpetual crest. The horizon loops away abruptly; a disc of earth, an island no more than a few miles long floating in the sky.

Suddenly, oil wells all around me. These well-head pumps aren't little ones, man-sized, like the ones I saw in Manitoba. These are several stories high. Everywhere I look they're bobbing up and down, the counter-weight turning with a heart-beat rhythm, rising, dipping, dunking and rising, sucking oil out of the ground. A good thing, too, because the land is scruffy, bleak. The farms, I guess they're ranches here, are huge. You can see the land fenced in for miles and miles without sign of house or barn.

Wherever roadways come out of these grazing lands onto the highway, rather than gates, there are simple breaks in the fence and a ditch covered with iron pipes set far enough apart that large animals can't cross them without their feet slipping through. Tires easily roll over them. Horizontal gates.

I'm getting a bit punchy from driving. Only been on the road about four and a half hours today, but I feel disoriented. I need a break. Stop soon — but not too soon. Got to keep moving.

Often, and I guess everyone feels it sometimes, I seem to be just off to one side, watching myself. More often when I'm upset about things: part of me seems to monitor my response, my behaviour. The worse I am, the more cynical this observing self becomes. I do not much trust myself at times.

It'll be good to visit Steve. He was at the reunion with Liz and her family a couple of months ago in Port Carling, but I haven't seen Carla in a couple of years. Don't really know her very well. She has the advantage on me, in that Steve would have talked to her about me, I imagine, but it would be quite, what — untoward — for us ever to discuss our wives. However open Steve and I may be as brothers, there are proprieties that sometimes grow as much out of tradition as loyalty, that are as well respected as not. The larger part of our lives is now away from the common family source.

• • •

Stopped for a break at a Gulf station. Was uneasy on my feet. Almost walked into a washroom wall. Decided to skip lunch. Make do with a small bag of chips and a large milk.

The chips are made in Cambridge, Ontario. That's what Preston is now called.

A few years back the Ontario Government forced an amalgamation of Preston, Galt, Hespeler, and the villages in the surrounding area of South Waterloo, including Blair.

Blair lies an open mile across the Grand River flats from Preston. The flats would flood every spring and when the waters subsided we'd

[81]

hunt carp in the pools, after school. Later, when the flats dried out, in shirt-sleeve weather, the earth still cool on the feet, we'd hunt morels, the tastiest mushroom of all; sauteed gently in butter, exquisite!

I remember eating more than one carp, scorched over an open fire. Taste of a scavenger lost in a dead still pool.

We've found morels near Bellrock. For twenty-five years I had gone without the taste of a morel and then a friend, Matt Cohen, let us in on a secret cache. People generally guard their morel grounds as close as a family scandal, and enjoy the special pain of sharing them the same way.

Spring for me is the marvelous sequence of gathering sap for boiling down to maple syrup, while the snow is still on the ground, followed in early May by gathering wild asparagus in secret places along the road-side, succulent weeds that escaped generations ago from cultivated gardens, and then in late May by morel season, when repeated empty forays are suddenly rewarded by a plethora of the delicious wild things, which appear overnight and in a few days are gone. Somewhere in between times we gather fiddleheads, curled shoots of fern which, steamed with butter, salt and pepper, are a gourmand's delight. We learned to eat fiddleheads in New Brunswick. We eat lily shoots and lily buds, violets, watercress, lambs-quarters, dandelions. Harvest in the summer and the fall is more domestic fare.

Potato-chips, a tinfoil bag.

It all seems distant now, my Waterloo County, Preston, Blair. Grammy lived at 231 Queen Street in Preston. Looking at the house from the front, the room with the bay window, upstairs left, is where Mom was born. She was married directly beneath, in the bay-windowed parlour, the same room that Grammy lay in, was laid out in, and Uncle before her, after they died. And my grandfather, too, though I don't remember that. Aunt Beth sold the house after Grammy died, it was too big for her alone. My grandparents built the house just before the turn of the century, barely in time for Aunt Beth to be born in it.

I lived there for a year.

Mom and Dad and five of us, in the house on the hill in Blair.

[82]

When I go there now, to Waterloo County, I am haunted by evidence of my forebears everywhere. What the old house, the factories and shops, the plaques in churches, Lynn Pattinson's name on the cenotaph (Lynn Pattinson died in the Great War; Clares and Mosses, Erbs and Pattinsons, all from Preston, fought in the Boer and the Great and the Second World Wars), what happens, what these things do is make me feel cheated, incomplete. All these, the people who precede me, on whose lives my life depends, are dead. I feel it as a burden, too, as if it's my fault, the price paid for me to be here.

I grew up with a full awareness of my kin in this place. When I was a kid, Clare Brothers Foundry was still a family concern; the Pattinson Woollen Mill flourished. Gone before my time were two furniture factories and a sled company, interest in an electric rail line and in a railroad to Lake Erie. Sixty years ago, separate families whose blood is merged in mine employed well over a thousand people in a town of about five thousand. I've grown up embarrassed to talk about this. And proud of it. Schizophrenic Tory. My mom's father was Mayor; his brother a member of the Privy Council, under Borden. George Pattinson was head of the Wool Board during the First World War and a Provincial Member for years, Minister of something or other, I don't suppose I ever knew, maybe I just made it up, but he was in the Legislature, I know that. Dad's uncle Frank Moss was involved in politics too. I remember at his funeral having Arthur Meighen pointed out to me.

There were carriages and gardens and gardeners. I have a card of my grandmother's, Dad's mom, Errington, who died just after he was born. "Mrs. Austin Moss/At Home/First Wednesdays." I don't think the phrase "at home" is actually on it. People knew what "First Wednesdays" meant. She was married only a short time. Dad was an only child.

The gardens, I remember some of them not yet overgrown when I was very young. Gardeners by then worked part-time after work at other jobs.

There were reminders all around me when I was a kid of people dead long before my time. Sometimes I think I have known these people, gone generations before I was born.

Grammy was/is a link with my past. Her memories of Preston reached back to the '80s when she came from Granton to work in the Post Office as the town's first telegraphist. At one hundred years of age

[83]

she could tap out messages in Morse Code on the maple arm of her chair, rapid-fire. Her father was a blacksmith and carriage-maker, her husband a foundryman. She was twenty-nine, I think, when she married Frederick Clare who, by then, was President of Clare Brothers, which had been established by his father and the father of Sir Adam Beck. Once, in a country restaurant, near Paris, Ontario, I saw an old Clare-Beck stove. They're a rarity. My family history seems dominated by men, yet it's the women I remember. Few of the men were left when I was growing up.

There were others in Preston, before the foundry and mill and factories — the Mennonites. My ancestor Johannes Erb founded Preston two centuries ago. His father, Christian, is buried there. "John Erb," my elderly aunts Ruth and Elizabeth call him, with more familiarity than, doubtless, he would have appreciated. His brothers founded Kitchener-Waterloo. I've Erb in me from both sides of the family and a little Mohawk, although that part is hard to document, there being a time when such things were hidden. It depends on who you talk to. There's no one left now who will say for sure.

I've never been interested in my ancestors preceding their arrival in Canada. Waterloo County is mine. Yet when I go there I'm a stranger, alien, haunted, between fear and pride.

At times it takes me by surprise, to realize suddenly I'm an adult. Often, I feel like a child inside. But it's not the child I once was, that I catch within myself; not reversion to the boy I was in Blair, with Erry a baby, Liz and Steve much younger, a war between us, and Rich, older. The kid I catch myself being has all that has happened since, within; a contemporary of me, now, an adult child. Not innocent: vulnerable; uncertain.

And yet childhood seems irretrievably out of reach.

Everything of the past is equidistant from the present; whether an hour ago, a week, or twenty years, located on a continuum only by thoughts associated with the recollection, not by the memory itself. Everything of the past is equally removed, equally inaccessible. Childhood seems another existence, all in a sequence imposed in retrospect, and I am allowed only vivid glimpses, passing by it on a train, peering

[84]

into the backyards of my life. Feeling perhaps I've been there, for awhile, unsure.

Only at about eighteen did the nature of retrospect time change substantially for me. Whipped out of line; into shape. The receding linearity of childhood almost suddenly gave way to an accumulating pool of experience.

Bellrock, no matter how close in mind, is past, now just beyond my reach.

Bellrock remains the centre I move away from and deeper into.

Bellrock, Ginny, Julie, Laurie, Paddy, Lady, Troy, Furry, Stripe. I say the names like an incantation. Geese, ducks, chickens, an androgynous rooster, garden, growing things, vegetation, trees, inanimate shapes, the rock, the soil, generic things, pine needles lying deep, alive in slow slow motion, alive the same way rocks are, all these alive within me now, alive.

Bellrock is a moving centre; moving away.

The ducks and geese are actually gone, given away to friends. The horses went to people who will care for them in exchange for riding. Paddy will go to the Mackenna's in Ottawa for the winter, when Ginny leaves.

Bellrock in my mind: the horses in the pasture, the geese and ducks squawking about in the bay behind the house. The images are authentic; this is the truth, if not the factual reality, of the present moment.

In the same way, the kids aren't just a snapshot memory of the way I left them, but the whole of our lives together, alive within. I do not carry their pictures with me.

Bellrock as I see it now has snow on the ground, deep and close

[85]

against the logs. The river is frozen over, the Volvo is parked on the ice out front, instead of discreetly under the ironwood tree in the pasture.

Bellrock is the smoke of a hardwood fire outside while the maple sap boils down to syrup in the early spring.

Bellrock is tumultuous with the explosive squeals of the kids swimming in the heat of early summer; fighting in play, testing the limits of what they can get away with.

Now I hear the sounds of Bellrock, the four of us lying side by side on the bedrock near the house one afternoon, distinguishing sounds one from the other in the country air; the sound of wind through dark green pine needles, a riffling breeze, the wind in the maple leaves, crisper, more liquid, hear it now. The water plays delicately against the rocky shore by our feet, slopping farther out around the elm piles that support the dock; hear it flow almost imperceptibly, and hear the cattle moving through the underbrush across the river, alders snapping, sucking hoofprints plashing; and farther, cattle in the fields whine imagined grievances, plodding hooves strike rock; and, from even farther away, the whine of truck wheels on pavement, on the Verona-Enterprise highway bypassing the village on the other side. Listen to the faint insistent cry of a whippoorwill, a killdeer's plaintive call from the pasture, the muted shriek of jays somewhere back in the island, the robins chirping defiance at murderous cats, a dozen other different kinds of birds singing in twelve-part harmony. One branch of the big maple rubs against the eaves of the house. Occasionally a frog or two, deep-voiced, muttering "Robert Reville, Robert Reville"; another, younger, higher-pitched, chimes in, "Clifford too, Clifford too." Listen, you can hear the waterfalls by Enid's, a rumbling so constant it could easily be missed; listen, you can hear us breathe.

Calgary soon.

Steve and I didn't talk much in Muskoka. There was so much going on, with Liz home from Australia with her husband and kids. I genuinely like my brothers and sisters, but when we get together residual affection will not always suffer the abuse of extended proximity. After a while all of us are anxious to get away and resume our own lives.

Liz has been officially Australian for ten years now.

I think it's difficult for her to realize that we haven't all experienced time passing in the same way, as a sort of compound phenomenon. It isn't that I now love my parents less, or my brothers and sisters, but that my allegiance to them and affection for them is in some ways fixed in time, like dried flowers in a favourite vase. Other complex loyalties and loves have grown.

Family origin is remembered consciously; ancestral origin is unconscious and must be learned. Grammy bridged these two. I had the great fortune to experience my origins, not only through documents and family lore, but in a singular person who herself knew people born in the 1700's. In three generations, with her in the middle, I touch the third century behind me.

six

For Erry, continuity with the childhood past has not been broken in the same way as for the rest of us, her life has not been re-shaped by marriage and kids. Her perspective on the past we shared is more direct and less obscured — and when the other four of us don't behave or respond the way she anticipates, it must undoubtedly be hurtful.

Erry and I are much alike in some ways. Combination of aloofness, and vulnerability.

Characteristically, Erry's lips seem poised, as if at any moment she'll begin to whistle an intricate tune, if only she can find the first note. Mine I hold, I think, casually apart, insouciant as I imagine it; or pursed, resolute.

At the Port Carling reunion, there were good times. Christmas dinner in July. Steve came but Carla didn't. Rich and his kids came, but Pat didn't. Someone who doesn't share in the root causes would

[89]

have to be highly motivated to tolerate such emotional confusion. Ginny came, by bicycle. Liz's husband, Nick, was there of course, along with the twins, Chris and Drew.

Memories. Apparently the same but in fact quite different for each. Contradictory.

This was a gathering of my parents' family. Julie and Laurie felt in some ways excluded.

There's such a difference with Enid's family, which expands spacially, as it were, to include us all, rather than being a patrilineal hierarchy or a diminishing line of descent. Partly of course, this is illusion, and sometimes I feel very much outside her family, looking in.

Shortly I'll be seeing Steve in Calgary on his home ground.

It's turning into a beautiful blue and white day. Drowsiness, a numbness in my head, crowding out coherent thoughts, words, my body's way of telling me to take a break, stop talking for a while.

forward rush, yellow line on the left, white line on the right

Driving by a lake off to my left; looks maybe fifty acres in size. It's a relief to see a body of water after all this land. Seem to have been driving endlessly with no water in sight except for a few rivers and creeks and the occasional salt pond — I assume that's what they are — rimmed with white sludge.

Getting into an area of Southern Alberta — stopped now for a train crossing the road — that could be Southern Ontario. Populated sections could as easily be a dozen miles from Bellrock, two thousand two hundred and eighteen point seven miles away. One tenth of the way around the world; at this latitude, even more.

Becoming quite compulsive about my recorder, spilling into it every random thought that passes through my mind.

[90]

Turn on the radio. That should do it. Nothing on but music. Here I am again (as if I don't exist, apart). It's my voice. Me speaking.

• • •

I've just recorded road noises for a minute or so, nothing more.
I see mountains.
They're still a long way off. In colour indistinguishable from the sky. They have solidity though, and dimension.

It's important to record the sighting at the actual time; when it happens. Not clock-time.

I'm crying . . . it's ridiculous, I didn't know I was so upset. I play back, replay. I say nothing.
Nothing's right now.

• • •

Had a good visit with Steve and Carla. Stayed for a light dinner, could easily have stayed all night, but I'm on my way. It's evening now, dusk, I'm on the four-lane divided highway connecting Calgary with

Banff, close enough to the mountains that they're beginning to assume bulk. The hazy colour takes on varied hues, they separate into receding planes. The foothills closer to me threaten to rise up and block them out of sight.

I wonder how it must have been for people travelling by canoe along the prairie rivers, or by horse or wagon, finally to see the mountains in the distance and then travel day after day after day, with the mountains only gradually assuming shape, slowly getting closer. The protracted joy at completing one phase of an arduous journey must have slowly merged with apprehension about what the mountains held for them ahead.

As I get nearer, they seem insuperable. My response is visceral, unexpected.

Dusk is cold steel blue. The sun slipped away without my realizing it, although a few wisps of fiery cloud remain high in the sky almost overhead.

I won't drive much further tonight. I feel more at ease in the mountains when I can see what I'm up against.

Steve was telling me about his adventures on a glacier climb last weekend. Such arcane pursuits hold little appeal for me — I did once want to jump from airplanes, but when a friend took up the sport, that was close enough — vicariously, it scared the hell out of me. I want at least the illusion of control over the terms of my possible demise. I thrill to the risk of things, where the danger and demands relate to wit or my capacity to endure. I've owned a motorcycle, which I cracked up in France, and I've jumped horses, shot rapids (smashed a canoe to smithereens once, no pride in that though), and swam farther, in rougher seas, than I was prepared for, scuba dived in fresh water and (eye-to-eye with barracuda), in the Caribbean. I love risk but I am not reckless, and have no wish to tempt fate in the sky or on mountain glaciers.

Steve told me about trudging along over the ice, attached by rope and harness to the other four in his party, when suddenly he plunged into a crevasse. Twenty feet down he stopped abruptly, dangling on the end of a safety line which had tangled in a knot around his chest so that his body weight suspended from his rib cage, and breathing was extremely painful.

I would have thought they could simply pull him out, but apparently it is a slow and cumbersome procedure, in order to prevent them all

[92]

from slipping in. The others had to sink anchors into the ice, then send a rope down to bring up his pack, then two ropes down with loops in the ends, one for each foot. Each rope was then hauled separately, one step at a time, while he shifted weight back and forth between them, so that he walked up through air, the deep-blue chasm falling infinitely below him. Incredibly, they had the ropes coming down from opposite sides of the crevasse. When they got him near the top, his head at surface level, he remained wishbone-like in pain while the others manoeuvred so that one side could gradually relinquish its hold while the other drew him up and over, where he lay exhausted in the snow for fifteen minutes, barely conscious.

The horror of it flickered across his face as he talked. Then joy, describing how they later sat on the snow up there eating lunch, seeing the real or other world far below. Pride mounted as he told of climbing up and over ridges of glacial ice along the sides of mountains.

My own survival I'd like somehow to relate more to me, to my own doing, or understanding.

I'm not a good flier. I don't believe in flight. In a plane, I suspect the absurdity of flight will suddenly prevail, gravity will be restored as a universal principle, and the plane will fall — not glide, but plummet directly to the earth and that'll be the end of it.

Oddly, I do quite a bit of flying.

Nearly dark now. Shadows soar high all around me. The highway stretches casually ahead, fades or drops or curves, indifferently.

Overlapping folds of darkness; still light in the sky high over the dark space I'm moving through; ragged edges of the planet, as if I'm deep in a hole beneath the earth.

Suddenly, off to my left, a cluster of vivid pinks, the first snow-capped mountains.

Today is Tuesday. Julie and Laurie will have gone back to school today, the summer holiday over. So self-absorbed that I forgot until now.

Funny, over the last few days I've thought quite a bit of them going back, feeling sorry that I wouldn't be there to send them off. Usually, I'm home to see them off, to tell them both as they leave, "have a good day," they kid me about that, invariably, "have a good day." I give them each a kiss and a hug at the door and tell them "be careful."

I won't be there to meet them after they get off the school bus and walk across the pasture and over the footbridge, along the path to the house. I won't be able to ask them, "Well, what did you do today?" to which they would reply, "Nothing much." Then, over the next few hours, in bits and pieces, the events of their day would emerge.

I was lucky to be building the house last year, so that I could be at home.

My God. They're asleep, in this same time as I'm in now. The sun set three hours ago in Bellrock.

I hope they had a good day.

Hope Ginny managed alright.

I'd like to be there, kiss the kids goodnight.

The last two months have gone so fast. The two months ahead, imponderable.

Go up, sit with Ginny, chat a while, read, when the News is over do some late night carpentry, work on the house, quietly to let her sleep.

I'm upset now.

Crying.

Thinking of them in the same present time as I'm in, now. Can't contain can't cope I'd like to be home to be tough to be done this drive this journey to be at the end of things I Jesus crying . . . .

Mad and crying.

Road sounds. Listen to the road sounds, rush of air, the engine breathing, heaving, whining tires, a quiet rush, listen to the road sounds . . . .

[94]

Nothing sobers a person like necessity. Suddenly, looming ahead, a Park entrance with what looks like a toll-booth. I assume composure, pull in to pay my fee, talk to the girl chattily, explain I'm driving through and won't be stopping, whereupon she lets me by, without charge. I'm sure that's what's supposed to happen, but I feel favoured anyway, as if she paid me a compliment, rewarded my self-containment.

Perhaps only the maniacal have such control. A curiously unrewarding thought.

Completely in control now. I think the best thing to do, to remain that way, is to shut off the tape machine and put it in the back and forget about it for the night and try as much as possible simply to shift my mind to disengage, where all I'm aware of are the practical aspects of driving through.

Dull and swarming, inarticulate feelings; random words and phrases. Transition. I'm giving birth to silence. Soon.

If it seems I never stop for gas or food or to stretch, it's because I'm not recording every move and mood and thought. The process is spontaneously selective; not a log book, more a chronicle. Leaving things out is a distortion. Still, there's no way I can put it all down; or want to.

Steve is a novice at mountaintrekking. Near the end of their third day, they were moving over the surface of the glacier; all of them including the most experienced were near exhaustion from what they'd originally described as, "Just a bit of a grunt over the ridge." Steve suddenly plunged through.

• • •

Stopped in at Banff for a coffee and to walk around. Scratched myself. Took a few deep breaths. Had my coffee black. Swivelled on the counter stool; would have spun, but didn't. Walked outside, scratched again. Tied my left shoelace tighter . . . my shoes don't have laces. Ha. Drove on.

It's ten now, but I've decided to make Lake Louise, or perhaps even Golden, British Columbia.

Ginny and I stayed at Banff on our trip four years ago. Walking around the town just now for half an hour I found myself thinking very fondly of Ginny, a warm nostalgia, thinking of things we do together.

Before I was married I travelled quite a bit. Usually on my own. But Ginny and I seem to share travelling experiences in ways that make the pleasures better. We're alive to each other, and volatile, unpredictable in our reactions, even after a dozen years of marriage. Our life together may be a strain at times, but it's never boring.

A year and a half ago we went to London, England. At Christmas Ginny came through with a staggering gift; using private money from her family, she surprised me with a theatre tour, a week in London for the two of us. I don't know how I could ever receive another gift to match that one for magnificence.

Other gifts, for different reasons, have meant a great deal to me. The most precious I think I've ever received was one Christmas when Laurie had just turned five and she gave me a little plaster-cast painted doll she had bought much earlier in the fall at a garage sale for a nickel (it was still marked in pencil on the bottom!). She had bought it for me especially and had hidden it away for Christmas because, when she pointed it out at the sale, I had agreed with her (casually) that yes I did think it was very pretty doll. I treasure that little doll as much as anything.

Julie makes things, beautiful things, from paper and cardboard and odds and ends, which she solemnly presents to us, declarations of affection. These things are born out of her own interior worlds, and often they are quite lovely. Pictures, miniature houses, carved elephants, sewn things; she did a pair of tie-dyed pillowcases for us that are exquisite. She is the most inventive person — I get mad at her but I admire her.

Our trip to London was on a scale I was hardly used to, nor prepared for, being out of graduate school only a couple of years. That one week we packed in so much it seems in retrospect like we'd been there several months. And, part of the illusion, like we'd only been there a flash of hours. We filled every corner of each day with shows and shopping, trips and touring, attending everything from Madame Toussaud's to Westminster Abbey to Canada House in Trafalgar Square. We ate exceedingly well.

I had spent good times working in London, fifteen years before, back when I was sure the centre of the universe could not possibly be in Canada, never mind a place like Bellrock.

I think I derived the most pleasure on that return trip from seeing the pleasure Ginny got from my responses. She was pleased for me and proud for having brought it all about. I showed her around London as if it were still my city. If I confront my memories directly, now, a lot of the loneliness comes back to me, along with the gnawing anxiety, being broke, working at menial jobs, sometimes hungry, always the foreigner outside the magic circle of belonging, always, never at the centre.

I did love London then, no question of that, but I never felt myself comfortably a part of it. I avoided other Canadians as much as possible, stayed away from other travellers, except when I lived in Earl's Court for a couple of months, when it was still the gathering place for wanderers from all over the world. In England I wanted to know the English. I lived in South Kensington, West Kensington for a while, and, longest, in Knightsbridge. I worked at Harrod's in the sub-basement, as a packer, and later as an electrician's mate at the Aldwych Theatre, the Royal Shakespeare. I lived in an attic room in Knightsbridge, five flights up. Shillings in the meter. Peeing in the sink. A bedsitter. Self-extinguishing light-switch in the hall. I took long walks alone in Hyde Park. Brooding, writing. Watching myself live an adventure.

Ginny and I were visitors, that was the whole point. We dined out, travelled by taxi, did brass rubbings in a church off Picadilly; one of them is hanging at Enid's and the other beside our bed upstairs in the log house where, I guess, where Ginny is now, where I should be.

Quick now, drive quietly. In the dark there's just the feel of my skin from the inside. If I think about it, my bottom's numb; my legs are sore; my knees ache. It's absolute black outside. Nothing to say I'm surrounded by mountains; only the idea.

· · ·

Lake Louise. The morning of my fifth day.

I'm amazed how anxious I was to get started again. While I was shaving and all through breakfast thoughts kept rushing into mind and sliding off again. I was tempted to make notes. Spontaneity is essential though, if I'm to get it right. Form is inseparable from the moving context, the immediate location of my mind, in process.

This morning, first thing, I played back a few minutes of the tape I made last night. The speaking voice was slow, drowning. With fresh batteries, the syllables burbled against each other, a strange and ragged whine.

Just crossed over into British Columbia.

What I thought I was putting in was not what I got back. I felt betrayed. Also, an odd feeling of fragmentation.

If the voice changes, what about the words? Do they convey what I said? I know they're mine in the present tense, as I spoke them. But as I play them back, time has passed, they're in a different present. Listening, I experience two quite different present tenses simultaneously.

— no word can mean the same thing twice, its context alters with every instant, the conditions of perception alter, every usage alters every word —

Imagine playing this back not five minutes or five months but five hundred years from now, how different it would be from what I intend, this being perhaps the sole evidence that I existed. Imagine me alive, still, an hour from now, or a decade, I will inevitably have changed, imagine then how disconnected I become from my words as they were spoken, lost to me I suppose even as I speak them.

Verbal language is unnatural; an invention of the species.

The joy of words, their infinite potential, lies in imperfection.

The challenge is to find equations which convey precisely from one consciousness to another the inarticulable.

Does what goes into this machine come back invention?

Words themselves exist no more than colour does.

[98]

My fifth day. It's Wednesday. Don't want to get all the way to Vancouver; I'd like to stop a hundred miles or so outside of the city and on the sixth day have an easy trip in.

And on the seventh day, rest.

Tomorrow, I'll go out to UBC for a couple of hours. There's much to do, getting ready for classes, finding a place to live, exploring Vancouver, getting the feel of things.

Back a way I passed a cave high overhead where Ginny and I stopped four years ago, just before leaving British Columbia, going the other way. Ginny stayed in the car and I began to clamber in what seemed no more than a ten-minute exercise up a grade of rough gravel and small sharp boulders to get to the cave entrance. Mountain distances deceive. Caves fascinate.

When I finally reached the opening I was exhausted. My knees hurt, threatening to buckle. I looked down at the car far below and waved at Ginny, waved more and more frantically because there was no response.

Waited twenty minutes for her to notice me then, crushed and wobbly, I began the descent, as if I had just scaled Everest before Hillary and Tensing, but there was no way to prove it. Ashamed of myself, that satisfaction and recognition were so totally entwined. At the car Ginny roused to greet me. "Did you have a nice walk? Did you get to the top?"

"No," I said. "Just to the cave."

"What's it like?"

"Okay," I said, "for a cave."

It was only a tenth of the way up the shoulder of the mountainside. I remember sulking until we reached Lake Louise for lunch.

There was nothing to the cave itself, an illusion of shadow, colour, and the contour of rock.

I've been driving with the window down for a while. The air has the crisp and penetrating smell of winter. So much in the midst of the mountains now I can only see horizon by craning down against the window and peering upwards.

This rocky planet surges high above me, jagged vertical planes overlapping one another. It's impossible to anticipate where the road is going after it disappears around each curve ahead. There seem no openings in the rock. The car moves tentatively. It's as if I'm descending into a great pit.

The brakes squeal on the downhill runs. I don't like to use a lower gear for engine drag to slow me down, though. Too much strain on the engine. It would be bloody hell for the car to break down here, in the middle of the mountains. I'd never get out. It would be bad enough to lose a tire.

I've come out into the open. Sky is visible. The highway cuts into a rock face along the side of a pass. The world is large again, a huge clear tilted hemisphere of sky. The mountains huge, nature using hyperbole.

For the first time this trip I feel acutely aware of being inside a bubble of metal and glass, removed from the world I'm travelling through. Sensations, such that if I were to close my eyes and open them, I might be anywhere. A witness only, passing by.

A whimsical notion: I could blink and all this would disappear.

I remember as a kid lying in bed, mourning that at my own death everything would go on, the same. Perspectives change.

Someday, the sun will die, time will collapse, it will seem that we have never been. That grieves me, now.

Perhaps nothing does exist beyond consciousness; our universe, something dreamt. If I awaken it will disappear. I, I become the dreaming man; I, the universe.

The only evidence will be the words I leave behind.

Steve pointed out that when he was a student in California he drove home for Christmas, twice as far as I'm going now, in an old Volkswagen with no heater, in the dead of winter. So how was my trip such a feat? Odd, because until then it hadn't occurred to me a feat at all, but a journey away, a separation, an emotional adventure, personal account, diary. Autobiographics: a novel-memoir.

[100]

seven

There's a black bear in the middle of the road! Strange to see it lope across, slow traffic to a halt, wander back again, leisurely, seemingly more tame than animals I've seen in zoos. Muscular and dirty, rodent-like. Lugubrious bear. The traffic, bored, starts up and eases slowly by. I can still see him, receding in the rear-view mirror, his back hunched, watching us.

Is it ideas and facts I want to get across? This is what I'll have to judge ultimately. Or is it the ambiguous nuances, emotional intricacies, which the facts yield up or, paradoxically, suppress?

Is what I intend conveyed by syntax and conscious intent; or is literate articulation merely artifact, implying a discontinuous vital complex other world, not otherwise accessible?

May spontaneous discourse be literate? Or is spontaneity itself an illusion, as illusory as meaning?

In this ambiguous Odyssey I am an artifact — I, now, here, creating — what? myself — as context, journey and protagonist.

• • •

I, a theoretic point at the intersection of a theoretic past and future, the theoretic present. Time, like words, has no being of its own.

One can only be, in imagination.

I can only be, in fiction.

Being is a paradoxical concept. Think about it.

To be, I must be fiction.

• • •

Sign for Rogers Pass, ahead. Climbing long steep grades. The car is slowing. The engine shudders from the strain, churns. At times the pavement edge drops off sharply so that you can see no bottom, only the land rising sheer, across the valley. I wish I had changed the tire.

[102]

The kids will be getting on the school bus now and Ginny will be drinking her third coffee of the morning and laying out her plans for the day. . . .

No, I've got that wrong. It would be later there than here. They'd be having lunch by now.

I have to think it out every time. The sun rises in the east, sets in the west.

Ginny organizes each day with meticulous care. At night, she's exhausted, but immensely satisfied if she has reached the point she anticipated in the morning. Occasionally, she gets depressed that tomorrow will bring only a new list of problems and projects to be strategically deployed throughout the day. She gets a lot done.

Ginny and I are both workers. I've always felt with me it's because I'm inherently lazy, and to compensate I drive myself especially hard. If I give in I might collapse in the middle of my life and not get up again.

Ginny, being more organized than I am, her periods of exhilaration and despair take on a more coherent rhythm than mine. I tend to sink deeper and deeper under the weight of projects, even recreation. I sink until I feel I'll break from the strain, and then something in me clicks over, a survival mechanism.

Once I had myself admitted to a psychiatric hospital, years ago, but after several days I decided that I'd better straighten up and get the hell out of there. I asked to be discharged, and since there seemed to be no reason to keep me (the most unbalanced thing I had done was to ask to be admitted in the first place), they let me out on what amounted to night-parole, wherein I slept at home and came in for the day, to sit around, mostly. After two days of this, I simply didn't bother going

[103]

back. No one inquired to see where I had gone. Perhaps I haven't been officially discharged.

That place though — my God, I can't see down. On the right, nothing, a sheer drop. No rail. On the left, I can only see to a shoulder of rock. Ahead, a wedge of brooding sky, chunky peaks of rock with snow flashing at the tops.

— the worst part was, after convincing reception late on a Sunday night to admit me, I was stood in an office stark naked for 45 minutes, waiting. People walked in and through, ignoring me, no longer a person. There was no chair, or at least I wasn't offered one. No window in the room.

Later, forty-eight hours in an observation room with twenty-nine other people, and exactly thirty beds. Lights on all night long. Excitement, fear, relief, I remained almost totally silent, by choice.

It was the fall of the year. Later than now.

Got much too upset last night.

Wallowing: self-pity is self-perpetuating.

I've got to keep, in perspective, everything.

Ginny has no option, given our priorities, but to stay in Bellrock until she finishes some research she is running, a continuation of her work at McGill. It's with pigeons, but perhaps it will lead someday to better treatment for children with dyslexia. What I'm up to at UBC is not of the same order. I've been teaching Canadian literature for several years now and I feel at ease in the field, but I'm not under any illusion that I'm heading for the coast to make a significant cultural contribution. I'm going because the academic year is about to start and I'm being fairly paid for it. I don't mean the literature isn't important. It is. In my judgement Canadian literature is an indispensable aspect of national survival, as well as of my own personal well-being.

I could have brought the kids with me, but that didn't seem sensible, really. This whole sojourn West is temporary and we want to make it as easy for them as possible. No matter which way, the separation will be upsetting, but at least they're on familiar territory, home at Bellrock, where they can better cope with it. They're excited about the adventure ahead, when we'll all be together again on the coast.

[104]

Sometimes travelling these crazy angles it's hard to tell whether I'm going up or down — except for the straining of the engine, its tendency to steel itself against the downhill run, to shudder on the uphill; and except near trees, seeing them reach directly vertical towards the sun.

The mountains I'm travelling through now, the ones I can see, remind me of the Laurentians north of Montreal. Not quite smooth-shouldered, but stooped, with trees struggling to the summits which, unlike peaks, shift depending on your perspective as you move around them. When we lived in Montreal we sometimes drove up into the Laurentians. Of course, our preference, because we then were only two hundred miles away, was to go to Bellrock on weekends and holidays. Perhaps Bellrock was too accessible for us ever to settle and feel at home in Montreal. The city was convenient, though — in some ways, that's what got to us. Convenience. It was difficult to feel self-reliant, accomplished, purposeful, in the city.

I find Montreal provincial and pretentious, puffed up with its own importance as a cosmopolitan centre — the effect of two major language groups living so close together, and understanding so little of each other. There are far fewer world influences in Montreal than Toronto or Vancouver, fewer immigrants; the population is static; alongside shiny urban renewal projects, corporate monoliths, and the like, much of Montreal is shabby, atrophied, moribund. Indigenous architecture is quaint rather than imaginative; for the most part indifferent to the natural conditions, as if dramatic winters and mountainous city landscape have no bearing on the shape of buildings, or on people's lives. It is a city the cosmopolitan world has passed by, so absorbed with itself that it hasn't noticed. Clinging to images of the swinging sophisticated life a tiny minority perpetuates, it doesn't notice the rest of the population is home watching a bilingual re-run of the Plouffes on television.

Montreal doesn't have the dynamism of Toronto or Winnipeg or Edmonton or Vancouver. And it doesn't have the charm, except in commercially polished ghettoes, of Quebec City, Victoria, Kingston, or Halifax.

Most Montrealers I've met, and certainly the media, resent Toronto. They seem pathetically competitive, and thoroughly intimidated that Toronto largely ignores them.

Steve and Carla were telling me in the West there is terrific resentment of Toronto, the East.

[105]

In the Maritimes we discovered that people would turn on us, as Upper Canadians, with bitterness hard to understand, an historical enmity held over from the act of Confederation, more than a century ago. Ginny found such antipathy oppressive, I didn't mind so much. I felt at home there and found the prevailing attitude towards Upper Canada, Toronto, increasingly comfortable to live with. Of course, you can't become a Maritimer. Not even in two or three generations. Either you're from there, or you're from somewhere else. But Fredericton was like the Southern Ontario of my growing up, twenty years earlier, as if time had paused for a couple of decades and then moved on at a slower pace.

An older lady across from us on Charlotte Street introduced herself our first week there. Frederictonians, in particular, can be so gracious as to immediately evoke other eras, when life was different than it is now. In mid-conversation with Ginny and me, her eyes lit upon the colour of our license plate, on the back of the car. She turned and walked away and didn't say another word to us the whole three years we were there. Didn't so much as acknowledge our existence if we passed her on the street. It was laughable and distressing at the same time. The kids didn't notice such attitudes, being still small enough (Julie was only three and a half when we went there, and Laurie less than a year) that they expected peculiar behaviour from adults as a matter of course.

Perhaps I felt at home because I kept apart from the community, an observer, and it's a very beautiful there.

Sunlight's trying to wipe the clouds away. The day is perking up a bit. . . .

Stopped at Rogers Pass to get gas. Chatted briefly with a girl riding a motorcycle through the mountains, I'm not sure in which direction. She had a small topless box attached behind her seat with a black and white dog in it, riding pillion. Seeing it like that, perched quite protected yet recklessly in the open, sent a lingering surge of excitement through me.

At times I can't help but wonder at how immensely ordinary my own life can be.

[106]

There's a glacier straight ahead, poised across a mountain ridge. It seems prepared to leap — although I suppose it's actually receding as we wind up this present ice age and anticipate the next. Animals will do that, project threat while in fact retreating.

Streams plummet straight down the mountain sides. You can see their origins in the ice banks above, and see them disappear into the valley far below. So extravagant in their energy, so much power, plummeting, so short a distance. You can see them whole, beginning to end, source to final dissipation in the common flow.

Just passed the first graffiti that really appeals, a message scrawled in vivid red on a cement bulwark at the entrance to a tunnel, eloquently simple — "Wendy Jean Fraser, I love you. Brian."

The summer we started to build the log house Laurie was a year and a half old. Julie was four and a half, not experienced enough to recognize the unusual, nor too jaded to delight in the ordinary.

Others were less tolerant.

Quite a bit of time Julie spent across the river with Enid where they shared arcane adventures of imagination born out of even the most trivial work around the place. A type of understanding grew between them, child and grandparent bound by blood, the gap of a generation filled with affection and mystery. That summer Julie and Enid discovered a special bond that will surely last them all their lives.

Sometimes I'm jealous of the intensity of Julie's relationship with Enid, yet I would not for the world want to diminish it.

A good part of the summer went to putting in a solid base for the house, building an insulated floor on the uneven bedrock. We had to rent a portable jackhammer to clear off a couple of outcroppings. For fifteen hours I hammered against the island, and, for three days after, the hammering continued inside my skull.

When it came to raising the logs we had our hands full. They were heavy enough to start with. While lying in the water for a few days when we floated them over, getting a preliminary cleaning we thought, the ancient dry wood sopped up weight like a sponge. We had to haul each log ashore to the building site, only feet away, using a chain-fall, and sliding them along a track of wetted plywood.

The car just shuddered violently for no apparent reason! Followed by a long sighing spasm from the engine. Don't know if the altitude might affect the timing. . . .

We raised the walls by building a tripod of logs out front, lashing log arms against trees on each side, and suspending a chain from high up in the maple at the back, then using the chain-fall to lift them one at a time into place. There is no way for heavy machinery to get over to the island, but with this system we managed quite well, although a few times the larger front and back logs, thicker each than a telephone pole, slipped over on us, and the tripod broke once, sending a thunderous pile to the ground and us into sudden nervous exhaustion.

Hardest to work with were the ceiling beams. Each weighed hundreds of pounds and there was no way of securing assistance from the chain-fall to raise them. I would lift an end, a bit at a time, and Ginny would slide blocks of wood under, until we had one end up high enough that I could get beneath it. Then, using my legs as much as possible, my back against the beam, I'd rise from hands and knees upwards until I held the end of the beam straight overhead, then together with a lot of groaning and heaving we'd walk it forward into the notched position on the upper log. Getting the other end up was heavier and more dangerous. We had to lift and at the same time push it backwards so that the high end wouldn't slip out and sent the beam crashing down on us, and we had to swing it sideways as we lifted in order to accommodate its full length in the confined area. We managed to get all six up with only one bad accident — one of them got away from us and smashed a hole through the floor, but it missed hitting us.

In the last week of the summer we raised the four remaining rounds of log, taking the walls up to the storey-and-a-half level, and securing everything for the winter as best we could.

The following summer we returned with two kids at the scampering stage. Laurie wasn't a baby any more. Being on an island, and me being a natural worrier, we had our hands full. (Now I wonder if they're more vulnerable because I'm not there to worry over them.) Our biggest fear was that Laurie would get up in the night and wander, with every direction leading to water. Ginny built a fence around the tent platform, with a gate we could lock.

That summer of '72 I spent most of my time building the roof while Ginny worked on the chinking. Since we had more time than money or sense, we decided for roof rafters to use old five by twelve-inch hand hewn beams we bought at the wreckers, ripping them down the centre to make them go twice as far. I used a gas-powered chainsaw. Day after day I fought to hold the bucking saw to a straight-line cut, until my muscles would scream from the strain and my head pound from the piercing whine of steel on wood. Finally done, the roof went up, with a gable built over the front door and broad pine planks showing inside over the labouriously worked rafters. Outside, sandwiching layers of styrofoam, plywood, and roofing paper, we put a covering of split cedar shingles. When it was time to go back to Fredericton for what was to be our last year there, I still hadn't closed in the end triangles between the top logs and the roof. That proved to be a mistake.

Ginny's chinking job was painstaking because the logs were crudely cut, the original builder's intention undoubtedly being to cover them with boards, inside and out. The original chinking had been mud, with horsehair as a binder, packed around lengths of split cedar cut to fit the irregular slots between logs which sometimes converge to touch each other and sometimes stray as much as six inches apart. She cut strips of wire lathe to shape and stapled them in place, using the same heavy-duty staple gun I used for the shingles, and then she applied a layer of cement varying to as much as one and a half inches thick as she shaped the chinks to relative uniformity. She's a meticulous worker and the over-all effect is of casual order, a finished look that is at the same time primitive; profoundly moving, to me at least, for what is revealed of craftsmanship and aging wood.

After doing most of the chinking outside, Ginny stuffed fibreglass insulation between the logs from the inside, along with blocks of wood here and there beside the cedar strips to help support the weight of the logs, so they wouldn't sag down over the years. More wire mesh was cut to fit, stapled, cemented. The walls took on substance; and a character new to them, unlike their old presentment to the world where they were disguised, hidden and then left to rot.

By the end of the summer she still had about a third of the house to go, so wind and weather could slash through the walls here and there in a random pattern, as well as upstairs, around the roof-ends.

We flew back that year to spend Christmas at Bellrock, a special treat. Crossing the ice a few days before Christmas we discovered the roof had collapsed: the front half lay flat across the top of the log walls,

[109]

while the back had slid over to the ground, taking the top back log with it, and lay propped recklessly against the back of the house.

I remember my eyes welling in the bright sunlight. Rage with no direction built up inside, alternating with calm resignation as I attempted to minimize the catastrophe, to play it down. Confused emotions for days. Despair lasted through much of the winter, gradually alleviated by mounting excitement at finishing our programmes at the University of New Brunswick, Ginny with her MA in Psychology and me with a Doctorate in Canadian literature.

When we returned to Bellrock after graduation and our trip west, we set about raising the roof. Somewhat surprisingly, with a bit of foolhardy ingenuity, we had it up and secured in a week. At one point, with the front part raised and held by supporting timbers balanced precariously on jacks, with me lying across on top working a lifting device known as a "come-along," with Ginny high in the maple hauling the whole back section, battered as it was, up into the air with the chain-fall — the chances of success seemed in direct proportion to the risks to life and limb. As Ginny hauled the roof section up, I coaxed it over across the retrieved top log, until finally it settled into place against the new ridgepole as neatly as if it had never been away.

Over the next few weeks I worked obsessively to secure the two halves together, anchoring the four corners with rods driven into the top logs, spiking cross braces cut from our own trees between every pair of rafters, building, in effect, a truss system, after the fact.

That summer and the next two, we worked cleaning off the logs with lye, treating them against bugs and rot, framing in windows and doors, refinishing old multi-paned windows and old doors. By mid-summer 1975 we moved out of the tents into the house, which we still called a cabin. Later that summer I ripped up the tent platform and we planted grass and a couple of trees where it had been. There's no evidence now that it was even there.

By the end of summer we had decided on moving to Bellrock to live the year round.

In the fall I resigned my job, effective the next spring. Ginny worked to finish her Doctoral residency at McGill. Once begun, the process of leaving seemed inexorable.

In May I took off for three weeks to France, to speak on Canadian literature in Rouen, where I discovered there was a Robert de Moss who accompanied William from Normandy to England in 1066. I also lectured in Paris, where I was threatened at knife-point on the Métro. On the way over I stopped in Iceland, where I was cold, and stayed for a few days in beautiful unfriendly Luxembourg. I also spent three days in Heidelberg, waiting for the minimum time on my excursion fare to pass so I could go home. I was bitterly lonely for Ginny and the kids, whom I had left in the midst of the extended transition from Montreal to Bellrock. That's the only other time I've been away from them for more than a few days. The pressures were different then, of course, and the period of separation much shorter.

Our house was still for sale in Montreal, and would be for another eight months. The Bellrock house was a finished home only in dream-potential. Determined as we were, there was a lot of uncertainty. In terms of real estate values, career moves, creature comforts, we had embarked on a dubious adventure. It was the wrong time for me to be travelling about the Continent, and never have I been so glad to be home from anywhere. My bags loaded with Le Creuset pots for the new kitchen. My briefcase stuffed with crude sketches, design concepts borrowed from Europe, encountered killing time.

As soon as I got back I started digging out the basement for the large addition, the kids' area and kitchen. We worked without formal plans, making it up as we went along, designing according to conditions as we met them, adapting to accommodate whatever whims and necessities we thought to include. On and off I also worked on the addition at the other end of the house, the library, to accommodate my grandfather's books and the large hanging quilt that Ginny and her mother had made the previous year.

Working back and forth from one structure to the other, on either side of the house, we managed to get everything weatherproofed enough to move in on Christmas Eve.

While the back was still a hole in the ground erupting with pine stumps, Ginny produced a truckload of planks a full two inches thick and fifteen inches wide, by twenty-five feet long, seventy years old or more, that had been part of an abandoned schoolhouse somewhere near Tweed. They were unfinished, rough-sawn. We had a three week interlude while we sanded these down smoothly, individually, for the floors. They stretch the full length of the log part of the house, a mellow gold beneath layers of urethane which protect them and draw out their intriguing depths.

Oddly, it took some getting used to when they were first laid in

[111]

place, because of their thickness. It was as if the windows had dropped and the ceiling descended a full two inches.

Digging the basement out by hand was difficult. The stumps were particularly recalcitrant, clinging to the earth and clay. By then we had a power hook-up, so while we poured the footings, laid the cement blocks that had to be floated over by raft, layered the hole with six inches of crushed stone wheelbarrowed across the bridge and along the path, and poured the foundation-floor, I watched the 1976 Olympics on television, live from Montreal.

Another interlude: from mid-September to late October, we dug the hole for a five hundred gallon septic tank; and a thirty-by -forty-foot tile bed, three feet deep; also by hand. Day and evening, days on end, I worked digging. Sometimes Stan and Truus Dragland, staying at the Ondaatje's up the road, came down and helped but it was very rare to have anyone else working with us. Ginny, who was still at Queen's part-time, helped when she could. Gradually, the hole expanded. The pressure was on to get it done before the frost closed in.

When the digging was complete, we were faced with the prospect of moving thirty tons of crushed stone from the pile under the ironwood where trucks had dumped it. Maybe a hundred feet by land, then eighty feet across a narrow foot-bridge, then another hundred and fifty feet to the cavity in the ground, under where the garden had been. I remember making a hundred and twenty trips in one day, the wheelbarrow loaded so full the tire was pressed out of shape as it moved along the rough terrain, binding on the bumps, roots, rocks, and soft mounds of needle-covered earth. Including one cold Saturday when we had the help of other friends as well, reinforced with a bonfire and beer, we managed to spread a deep bed of crushed stone in minimal time. After laying the pipe we brought over more stone to cover it and to pack against the feeder pipe that runs a hundred feet from the house to the tank.

By this time, night-frost lingered well into the day. I was increasingly apprehensive that we couldn't get it filled in before the ground froze solid, and we would be stuck without sewage disposal until spring. As Hallowe'en loomed closer, we began shovelling earth back in, the earth clinging to the shovels in frozen clumps, then suddenly slipping off, wrenching expectant muscles. We covered the tile bed over with the three feet that we had scaled off it, and in the early spring I brought over a couple of tons of horse manure by wheelbarrow, courtesy of

Lady — we didn't have Troy yet — and the area reverted to the role of vegetable garden. Largely Ginny's domain. I don't have the patience.

Gardeners and builders are not unalike. Both need faith and a vision. They work for a future they cannot see but only imagine as completed, they believe a nail or a seed will become something else, a whole thing. But gardeners need patience, for much of their work is done waiting, nurturing; they weed and water and provide an optimum environment. Building something, I make it grow; and if I stop, it stops.

In spite of the relative lack of sun due to the high surrounding pines, vegetables seem to flourish under Ginny's hand. Some, of course, better than others. Peas and tomatoes and lettuce do the best.

Once the septic system was finished I got back to the carpentry. By this time, Blake Cox was there doing the wiring and the guys from Verona Hardware were installing the plumbing for the bathrooms, laundry, and kitchen. The best break I've ever got from Verona Hardware was the cheerfulness of their working habits. We didn't qualify for a builder's reduction, building the house ourselves, but, generally, suppliers were very agreeable. Sometime earlier, Ginny and I decided we wouldn't try the plumbing and electricity because time was increasingly at a premium if we wanted to move in before winter. At this stage of things we were no longer intimidated by taking on such unknowns and the wiring in particular offered a bit of a challenge, but when cold first set in we had moved over to Ginny's mother's place and were anxious to get back on our own. The Montreal house had not yet sold but still promised to cover such extravagance, even though Levesque's separatists were by then in power and real estate prices had dropped drastically. We were optimists.

On the 23rd of December last, 1976, I worked through until 5:30 in the morning. The electric heaters were turned on full blast and still my fingers froze, brittle and numb, as I placed bats of insulation in the walls and ceiling, determined to move in and spend Christmas in our own house. The 24th, Christmas Eve, we spent with my parents up in Waterloo County, in a ritual extending back to my childhood Christmases which coincided with Grammy's birthdays, when the extended family would gather, generations and generations of us, and Grammy the last survivor of her generation. How many of us who were there each year have gone now! When Grammy died the continuity was broken. But still on Christmas Eve we go back to Waterloo

[113]

County if we can, to be with my family. Christmas Day we spend with Ginny's.

After we got back from the long drive home, late on Christmas Eve, Ginny and I each carried one of the kids; we walked through a dark moonless night over the ice, and in through the library door, into the darkened house, and set the kids down by the Christmas tree; flicked on the electric lights, a miracle, it seemed, where there had never been steady dazzling light before but only the glow of kerosene or the hard glare of a Coleman lamp; flicked on the lights of the tree, and turned the others out. The kids were roused now by the excitement of Christmas out of the depths of their sleep and we sat together on the floor, the four of us, and sang in quiet voice the Christmas carols we loved the most, Silent Night my favourite and Little Town of Bethlehem, Away in the Manger, Good King Wenceslas, what we could remember of it. No secular songs like Rudolph or Jingle Bells that night, but quiet joyful songs, though none of us is religious.

Ginny and the kids let me sing with them. I kept my voice quiet and low, so that I could enjoy the illusion that I shared their harmony.

After a while we carried the kids upstairs and tucked them into our bed. Their room wasn't ready yet. Ginny and I unfolded the bed in front of the fire, which by now was dying low to embers. After a while we switched off even the Christmas tree lights and lay there holding each other in this home we were building ourselves and drifted off to sleep.

When the kids came down in the morning, everything was as if we had always been there. We went in to open presents under the tree and we were very happy together. . . .

It seems far away now,

from here, now, driving.

[114]

During the rest of the winter and into the spring I did carpentry work indoors, finishing ceilings and some of the walls in cedar, building cabinets and bookshelves. Ginny worked plastering above the cedar wainscotting in the kitchen and on the rest of the walls, working the plaster to a rough textured surface that fits perfectly with the extensive use of woods, the stonework and chinking.

During the past summer much of my time was spent putting up board and batten siding (I didn't quite finish, there's still a part around the kitchen, in the back, that isn't done), and shingling the new roofs with cedar shingles — we got through the winter with an underlayer of roofing paper. I was putting in three or four hours a day writing, Ginny worked at her garden which flourished, we had the animals to care for, the horses to ride, bees to tend, things to do. The evening before I left — it hardly seems possible that that was just last Friday, less than a week ago — I finished shingling over the back porch after the sun had set.

Ginny's got her research to do: The library is temporarily a laboratory with banks of costly and complex equipment. The kids to care for: I hope she enjoys this time, the three of them on their own. I know when I've been away before, for much shorter periods, they can be enviably inventive together, getting up to all kinds of adventures.

I hope Ginny finds someone to help her when she takes the supers off her bee hives. They're heavy now with honey that should be extracted before she comes away. She'll have to bed them down before winter.

A couple of weeks ago she had me working with them and I guess I was pretty cocky — she's the expert, but I figured the real secret to working with bees is in your attitude. That may be right, but I had the wrong one. Although I was wearing a face net and gloves, I had work jeans on with holes in the knees, and a couple of loose shirts and, I think, running shoes. When I found some ants inside a cover of one of the hives I started banging it on the ground to shake them off. Ginny called from about thirty feet away for me to stop, and to use the smoker. I didn't: implicit in the marital relationship is a stubborn resistance to the other's advice. As I reached over to place the top on the ground beside the hive, a cloud of bees swarmed around me. I was determined not to panic. Since the hive was still open with one of the supers on the ground, and possibly to save face, I kept on working; slowly now; paying attention to Ginny's running instructions. All the

[115]

while bees were crawling through where the netting had slipped away from my helmet, and working their way through the holes in my jeans and between the buttons on my shirts, and up my pant legs. I couldn't distinguish separate stings. I finally got the hive closed and walked away from it, walked in a random pattern, gradually losing the bees around me, some of them bitterly persistent. I crossed the bridge to the pasture and slipped off my clothes. The backs of my knees were furred with stingers ripped off kamikaze workers, with remnants of their abdomens still attached, some still throbbing. My chest bristled with stingers. More on my arms. My face was blotched; shooting pains in the back of my neck; burning in the small of my back. Ginny patiently scraped away at the stingers with a hive tool, sliding them out without squeezing more poison into me, one at a time. . . .

In all I had over a hundred stings. Surprisingly, after the initial burning died away I felt nothing more than a rush of lightheadedness. Ginny received a sting close above her eye and it took three days before the swelling subsided.

eight

Less than two hours now from Kamloops, in the heart of the interior.

The countryside here is appealing — rolling hills that build slowly off in the distance into mountains. Not looming stupidly the way the jagged snow-capped peaks did, back along Rogers Pass. Here there are trees and grass growing. The land has character you can relate to. I can imagine living here. Perhaps we'll take a trip sometime and come back through this way, perhaps drive to Calgary to see Steve and Carla. I'd like to show Julie and Laurie this country. I'd like them to see all of Canada, know their frame of reference. Give them a perspective on the world they'll encounter through the years they grow away from Bell-rock.

One's frame of reference I suppose is also one's point of departure. Bellrock isn't where I'm from, but what I'm from, who I am, and for a while at least it's also that for Ginny and for Julie and Laurie. If someday the kids have their own version of Bellrock, in some way that I can't reach or understand, I hope it is as substantial to their lives, as much their centre, as it is mine.

The air has a clean and hazy feeling to it. I think I'll sit back inside myself and relax a bit.

It's infuriating how people drive along and absently let their speed dwindle way below the limit, but when you go to pass them they're jolted into attention and accelerate, with you in the passing lane, and there you go, neck and neck, racing around a curve or over the crest of a hill, you in the danger lane. You don't know whether to force on or fall back. The incident I just worked my way out of: a downhill slope just around an inside curve gave me the edge and I crept ahead without excessive strain on the engine. Immediately as I passed him, he fell back, almost out of sight now in my mirror.

Must be careful not to praise the Volvo unduly at this stage; don't want to tempt fate.

There's a frontier quality to the homes and buildings here, the way gardens and pastureland are slipped into the scenery and enclosed by it.

Going up a steep and endless slope right now. The engine bucking somewhat, choking a bit. Making it. Now over, the engine settles.

From here to Kamloops I vow to say not one more word.

Ridiculous, the silence.

[118]

Woke up last night in the middle of a dream that I was someone else. Almost immediately the other self began to slip away from me. I had a lingering affection for it, but as thinking brought me more and more awake, elusiveness turned to confusion and the other was lost with certainty. Still I felt it might come back to me. This man or child or young woman, a slender young woman — that image seems comfortable to me now as I recall, but I can't be sure. I lay awake thinking what a good idea for a short story, *The Man Who Dreamed He Was Someone Else*, in a series of recurring dreams the other self becomes more and more defined, dream reality extending into wakefulness, first as substantial memory, then imposing personality, and finally displacing the waking self. Obsessive, madness, birth through imagination. I create people in my dreams. Perhaps one of them will become me; or uncreate me. When I went back to sleep, if she returned I don't remember. I awoke from a dreamless void, a slow rising into consciousness of myself.

• • •

Our private knowledge of love and death, not of good and evil, surely distinguishes us from each other.

I find myself apprehensive, tremulous inside as if I've crossed into forbidden territory.

Tonight I'm phoning Bellrock. I'll let them know how I am, let them know I'm safe and how I miss them.

We agreed before that we won't get upset on the phone. That would make things too difficult.

[119]

The other night I talked to them from Northern Ontario. Only Laurie gave in to a short plaintive sob before taking control of herself. Even at seven she realizes that that is how we help each other cope. Great passion can lie behind restraint born out of consideration. Reticence and dignity are not antithetical to passion. It may be that they eloquently assimilate it and convey it privately to those closest to us.

We four don't hesitate to express our love for each other, but none is so foolish as to think the expression is equivalent to love itself, which is a deep abiding thing beyond articulation.

Even when we are infuriated, there is never doubt that beneath the anger or hurt is a solid foundation, inexpressible and profound and wonderfully sustaining, a condition where our whole selves somehow merge, each with the other.

Death: I cannot bear to think of death except in contexts totally dissociated from the kids in particular. Ginny and I, somehow, I feel, are more able to cope . . . for myself, I think of dying rather than death.

Going down a huge steep hill, the brakes, the talk of death, absurdly terrifying, there's nothing wrong, the land flattens out, I survive for a while longer.

Enough of this, of death and love.

It's interesting, driving along the southern shore of the Fraser River, that I can see different weather systems at the same time. Across the river and down a long valley gorge it is clearly raining. Sky is slate grey-blue, seems to sag down to meet the rising land. Straight ahead, along the river valley itself, the sky is crisp blue and the clouds are grey, flashing with white around the edges. Behind me, in the rear-view mirror where I've come from, the clouds rise in great cumulus dumplings high out of sight overhead, benign and, paradoxically, threatening. To the left, it is clear blue with wisps of white leading off down another valley. The rolling hills here are huge, like those around the north-east corner of Lake Superior, but not so bushed over. Right now I can't see any snow-capped peaks at all. I feel at best a witness. If it wasn't for an overriding sense of nationality in the abstract, I think

I'd find this an alien setting. If I were a few hundred miles to the south, travelling through Washington State, foreign territory, I'd understand this estrangement from the landscape much better.

I have an abiding sense of Canada as geography, more so than as a political or cultural entity. So even when the land seems strange to me, and I, separate from it, I still have a certain feeling of being at home. I lost that feeling for a while soon after we moved to Montreal. I had grown up thinking of Quebec as part of Canada. Travelling through or visiting, it always seemed as much my world as the Maritimes, the West, the North. Yet, living there, in difficult times, I found that in so many ways Quebec and Canada are mutually exclusive, that Canada was surrounding us. Containing us. If I were Quebecois, I would be separatist, not a René Levesque quisling, but an out-and-out separatist. If I were a genuine Anglophone Quebecker, I'd be grievously torn between leaving my ancestral home or staying to fight for my ancestral rights.

Just passed a sign that said the South Thompson River. What I thought was the Fraser must have been the Thompson all along. These names, Thompson, Fraser, are names from school textbooks. Names I've always known, it seems, and even though I've been through here several times before I find them confusing, applied to real geography, outside textbook contexts. Names here are no longer things in themselves, for me. Now they're just labels, words diminished to meaning.

Gardens and fenced pastures sprawl irregularly across the terrain, here. Gestures.

Entering Kamloops. Suddenly from nowhere it's pouring rain. Pathetic fallacy has taken over — the engine chugs ominously, churns, the car shudders as we move along, not from the worn tire but from the violence in the engine itself. When I slow down the noise is louder. My two working pistons have marvelous tolerance. I have to think that way, and keep on.

The sign is deceiving. I'm still ten miles outside the town. The hills here are high and bare, scrub grass, a smattering of trees that seem almost blemishes; hills like dessicated skins flung carelessly over huge piles of rubble. I suppose that sinister image echoes Sheila Watson's haunting novel, *The Double Hook*. This land evokes the image I share with Watson; perhaps invokes it.

I've largely culled literary thoughts from consciousness, as I've been driving. It would be too easy to get involved with writers and their

[121]

works, brought in a steady stream to mind, obscuring my own responses; to use literature inadvertently as a buffer to keep me comfortably away from whatever it is I'm really trying to get at.

If it wasn't for my literary interests, though, I wouldn't be driving across the continent now, and I probably wouldn't have Bellrock, not the way we do. And surely my responses to the country I'm crossing, however indirectly, are deeply affected by my literary experience, by literature.

This highway climbs interminably as it arcs around Kamloops. The car slows gradually. Been on a steep incline for three or four miles now. I didn't know hills could be so high. And there's more to go.

My God it just goes on and on.

Finally cresting.

No, there's more. Have to stop soon. Breathing, heart beating, both to the rhythm of the engine pounding, as if my effort will reinforce it, help us up and over.

We're cresting. Hit the top. We're rolling, rolling over into a gentle downhill slope.

We're high here, but the hills still rise above us to the south, much higher. I can see a school bus, a tiny orange block, climbing almost to the top a mile or two away.

We'll stop the next chance we get and take a breath. We — the car, and me. I've been speaking plural.

Ponds along the roadside look like they're frozen over. Even as high as we are, here, that can't be ice yet. They must be salt ponds. I'll have to ask someone when I get to Vancouver. Some of my students will be from the Kamloops area. They'll know.

The last lap now.

Driving alongside a very narrow gorge: incredibly, there are houses down there at the bottom. How anyone could live there is beyond me. Their windows in every direction look into banks of earth rising steeply around them. Perhaps it makes them feel secure, out of the sky's reach.

I'm in a rainstorm. Quite suddenly. Parts of the sky are still blue, and yet the rain is thudding down on me and bolts of lightning flare in the southwestern sky.

[122]

Chunks of stone poke through grass covering on the hills. I think I'll soon be in mountains again.

Sex. It just occurred to me how little thought I've given sex over the last five days.

Perhaps there's a correlative between driving and impotence. It would be revealing to survey the private lives of truck drivers. Perhaps they cultivate their macho image in compensation.

Whimsy. But normally I'm sexually aware. It's odd. I guess what got me thinking about it was passing a young woman hitch-hiking back near Kamloops. She's the third woman travelling on her own I've passed, all going the other way. If she were going my way I would probably have picked her up. I'm conditioned enough by the clichés about women travelling alone that the possibilities are vaguely exciting. In the same way chatting with an attractive student, or a waitress in a restaurant, can be pleasant and unsettling.

I remember some time ago talking to a writer-friend about the sexuality of writing, the intense intimacy with oneself, which is loneliness only when creativity is at a low ebb, and rises to rapture when things go well. Didn't mean this in any Freudian sense, that punching the keys or clutching the pen equate with coital motion. But at some level there is sexuality about the creative process, when one establishes rapport with oneself, or selves one does not even recognize. Rapport, conception, gestation, labour, and finally the creation has its own life, apart from its creator.

My head is swimming, I've been driving now for seven-and-a-half hours with only a couple of brief stops. These roads are nerve-wracking. Head's spinning. Mountains here like huge huge hills. Inversions: the tops are tree-covered and the lower-slopes are barren, with only coarse grass and scruff bushes nubbing at the sides.

Concentrate on driving for a while.

I'm tired. The wipers slapping back and forth in front of my face don't help. Not sleepy though. Just sore, lightheaded . . . must be after eight in Bellrock. Odd, I have no idea what time it is here right now. Not sure what time zone I'm in. I know where the minute hand should be but not the hour hand.

It's a quarter after.

nine

Two hundred and twelve miles to Vancouver. If the car broke down now, I could almost walk it, and be there in time for classes Monday morning.

Somehow I haven't made the leap yet, to picture myself lecturing again after a year and a half away from it. Not like being on an extended sabbatical, where I'd know I'd be going back. I left with no return planned, although somewhere in a back corner of my mind I knew eventually I would. I like teaching. And I knew my writing wouldn't bring in enough.

Even after I agreed by telephone to the UBC appointment, the actual return to lecturing didn't take on the full force of reality. What loomed increasingly large was the coming separation from Ginny and the kids.

Now on the road I seem to be defining myself only in terms of what

I'm moving away from and not what lies ahead. I envision myself in Bellrock still. In my mind I haven't left there yet. I look in the mirror and my eyes transfix themselves, unmoving. I do not see myself here, so much as imagine myself.

Stopped raining. A brief hail came and went. It's a crabby looking sky. The road is slick and wet.

I suppose when I get there things will of necessity resolve themselves; things do. There's not much point anticipating problems, social or practical or, especially, psychological, nor anticipating their solutions.

This morning when I got dressed I put on my new jeans, saving the worn pair for tomorrow when I get there. I wonder how much more I'm doing in preparation, without thinking about it.

Passed a tiny cemetery at Spence's Bridge. Stones seemed miniature, smooth, not shiny, a number of them inexplicably painted rest-room green, perhaps they were, they must have been, wood markers, silvered by weathering, the green on them a preservative, or lichen.

Stopped at a station for gas and coffee. Watched a man down the counter from me with sordid fascination. Picking at himself, absently setting the retrieved detritus between his teeth which he ground until the action was lost in effort devoted to another search; devouring himself in an endless ritual of self-abnegation.

Bought a box of Cracker Jack as I was leaving. Haven't done that for years, for myself. Occasionally I've bought some for the kids and sneaked a few bites. Inside there is a 3-D card picturing an endangered species, one of a series.

It's a wolverine. Tuck it into the glove compartment for the kids.

Something running through my mind a lot; I've resisted saying it, making it real. Sometimes it passes through my mind that this account could be a legacy, a last testament, that something will happen to me, and these tapes will survive, for Ginny and the kids. I'm not sure where the idea goes from there. Suddenly, saying this, I feel threatened: ghoulish.

There will be time, before death, to speak with eloquence of love and understanding. Macabre fantasy. Playing morbid games. The difficulty I have articulating a genuine sense of foreboding is, itself, unsettling.

. . . the reason for all this would be clarified by disaster . . . bizarre . . . if I were dead, more would be communicated . . . . form and purpose, sanctioned by my death. . . .

[126]

I forgot to check at the service station on the time. I'm still three or four hours out of Vancouver. Seventy-eight miles from Hope.

I want to get off such morbid lines, but, suppose, afterwards, everything in the car was returned to Bellrock and they listened to my tapes and they found the card from the Cracker Jack box; it would connect them with the immediacy of my death, my present a presence to them, then . . . in a sense it sets me at ease. Listening to the tapes, hearing me speak in the present tense to them directly, life happening to me as I talk, they might be able to relate to what I went through in my last few days, they might better cope with the accident and the changes it will bring to their lives, to Bellrock.

The sun is a gigantic silver ball, the clouds unruly, the horizon soars against a fine silvery mist spreading everywhere. Fraser Canyon. Behind me silver turns to gold, such alchemy with light exhilarates, and ahead, now, the clouds turn solemn slate and swallow the mist, descend to earth, hang sullen and ponderous, indifferent as I approach.

These curves carved along the canyon side throw the car weight heavily from side to side.

A maroon Model T Ford just came rushing past me, out of nowhere. It must be doing sixty; the road is treacherous. Two mounties passed, going the other way, laughing.

I can see the Ford about three bends and a half a mile ahead along the canyon wall. Can't believe a car built before I was born could command these roads better than the Volvo.

Can make out an arc of highway for about a mile. No sign of the maroon Model T. He's either so far ahead I'll never see him again, or he's gone over the edge into the clouds below.

I'd just as soon this part of the journey were over.

Been going downhill, must be near the bottom now — just caught sight of the river, still a long way down. It's raining hard. There aren't any guard rails to block my vision, looking down.

Oh God! The traffic's stopped ahead —

Construction project. Don't know what I expected. Maroon fragments?

[127]

Just passed another tiny cemetery with those small marbled-wooden crosses. The cemeteries along here often don't seem to be located near communities. It's been half an hour since I passed through any place at all. Little cemeteries along the highway with little white fences, seem to belong to no one. The graves of railroad builders? Highway builders? Hitch-hikers? Victims of automobile accidents?

In the Indian cemetery at Bear Island, years ago, I remember seeing a small hand-lettered marker on a young woman's grave, and a childish paper rose beside it, made of Kleenex, with lipstick garnished petals . . . .

I don't know where in hell it came from but that Model T just passed me again! Clearly not an unmolested antique. Not a Ford; an Essex. Chopped and channelled. The person who did it has integrity; he or she maintained the sense of the original lines, what they should have been, if not what they were.

Still no guard-rail. Can't see anything when I look over, only the far wall rising away from me out of an abyss. I'm not sure I want to come here with Ginny and the kids. We could take a trip to Vancouver Island, or down to San Francisco.

Rain is heavy now, it streams across the pavement: each time I hit a sheet of water the tires seem to rise, lose contact, hover, the car threatens to spin-out, then the treads sink through again to pavement and the car swerves almost imperceptibly back on course, steadies, gathers itself again, rolls on, with me hardly in command, wishing more and more the sun were shining. If I go over, I'd rather do it in nice weather.

What a dismal day to die.

No, says Liz with her acquired Aussie accent, Yester-die. What the hell! Dumb joke.

It's funny how when Liz and Erry are around I confuse their names with Julie's and Laurie's. In many ways my sisters to me will always be kids.

It's the names, the labels, I get confused, not their identities. Each is unique in my mind. It would be wholly impossible to confuse Julie and Laurie with each other, never mind with anyone else.

No love compares in depth and simplicity with the love I hold, in common with every parent perhaps, for my own children. My love for Ginny is profound, awesome at times, but complex and ambiguous, occasionally baffling. My love for Julie and Laurie is simple and complete.

[128]

With Rich and Steve, Liz and Erry, there are strong bonds extending back to, and of course, beyond, the time when I left home, at seventeen, to live with Grammy and Aunt Beth and Uncle Tom in Preston, where I did my last year of high school. I was never home again, after that, except to visit. Not until Ginny and the kids and I made our own.

Ginny would be my executor if anything happened to me while she was still alive. Until now I've always assumed, without thinking much about it rationally, that, if I went, so would she. Our lives seem so irrevocably interconnected.

If I'm not careful I'll turn this into a bloody last will and testament. I'm not depressed right now. Content, in fact. Chatting to myself.

Richard introduced me to so much while we were growing up, so many memories seem to include him, particularly of discoveries: the taste of root beer; a cigarette; crawling in winter across the roof to watch the baby-sitter have a bath long before I was interested; hunting frogs; eating frog's legs; saving matchbooks; reading Classics Comics; listening to the Heavyweight bouts on radio, Louis and Walcott; listening to Lux Radio Theatre, Suspense, Our Miss Brooks, Baby Snooks. Rich was always there.

The rain stopped without me noticing it. I'm on the verge of laughing out loud. That scares me a bit.

[129]

I've seen a number of log houses along the route. Just passed another one. Quite different from ours. For one thing, they're far newer. Most log houses I'm familiar with are reconstructions, dating back to the 1840s or before. They're larger, the houses I know, than these, having been raised by groups of settlers working communally in building bees. These seem the work of individuals. In that, I feel more akin to builders here.

Battle Rock Tunnel, a nice name.

We've never talked about building with logs to other people who have done the same, either reconstruction or new. We talk between the two of us, of course, all the time. We've talked to people who have had the building work done for them, and we've read a few books and articles on the subject. Essentially we've worked in isolation.

I never remember the names of things. I either forget or don't bother knowing them in the first place. Tools, parts of the house, processes. I get joists and plates and trusses, sills and rafters, hopelessly snarled in my mind, even though I've worked my way through them all and could tell you exactly how any single part of our house, any part of it, was built. I know every hidden board and nail in that whole house.

It's interesting; often people who visit us treat Ginny and me as if we didn't really build the place — Ginny is the victim of this more than I am, because they tend to assume her role must have been secondary, supportive, a maker of coffee and sandwiches. Yet, in fact much more of her work shows than mine. Sometimes I feel slighted, but never jealous. So much social bias works against her getting the credit she deserves, I take great pride in due notice of her achievement.

Critics of our life-style tend to blame me more than her. Ginny seems so eminently rational about things. But it has taken the two of us together to merge the fantastic and the practical, to realize our Bellrock dream, and we both generate some of each.

When people visit us they often have difficulty reconciling what we've done in Bellrock with the people they think us to be.

They often treat us as if we too were visitors.

Slowing down to go through Hope.

• • •

Stopped for a coffee. Something was gnawing but not until I pulled in did I realize that whatever the time here it must be past the kids bedtime at home and I had promised to phone.

Ginny answered immediately. Julie and Laurie were in bed, but it wasn't long before Julie got on the extension. She said she made herself stay awake. Laurie tried, but fell sound asleep. I asked Julie to give her a hug and a kiss for me. Julie said she would tell her I sent them, but no way was she going to pass them on. Blech!

Ginny told me a woman in her late sixties turned up yesterday at the front door and said her grandfather had been born in the house when it was still on the hill over by Croyden. Would Ginny mind if she looked through? She must have been a cousin of old Mr. South. When Ginny showed her upstairs, she pointed to the corner where our brass bed now stands and declared it the exact same place where her grandfather had been born, and a lifetime later had been laid out, after hc died. I could hear the woman's voice as Ginny talked. And Julie chimed in, with a quaver, that she and Laurie were sleeping in the brass bed while I was gone.

Julie knows that this house has had many lives pass through it, most of them anonymous to us, but real and lived, nonetheless. I think she's proud of participating, the same as Ginny and I. Laurie is still at an age where ghosts are eternal and frightening, not sadly fading away in time, like smoke from a burnt-out fire.

I wonder if the people who owned the front door will ever come to visit, to see what we've done with it? We were driving around Enterprise last year after an auction and we saw this handsome old door hanging out of place at the side of a cement-block garage, so we, I should say Ginny since I waited in the car until she made contact, approached the people and asked if they would sell it. Sure, they said, and when I offered twenty dollars for the poor old thing, paint chipped, panes broken, some of the decorative trim cracked off, they took it, in obvious wonder at our naiveté. By the time Ginny finished scraping it down and repairing it, and I had enlarged the door frame to accommodate it, the door seemed, and seems, in perfect harmony with the house, as if it had always been there.

Ginny assumes if a door frame needs changing or a window should be added or altered in shape or size, that I'll cope, and she's usually prepared to put up with my griping as the necessary price.

I thought of staying in Hope for the night, but talking to Ginny and Julie, I felt unsettled and wanted to get back on the road for a while.

Pavement is nearly dry. Sky in the late dusk is grey. The sound of the tires on the pavement, soothing. Sounds of pistons are erratic enough to insist on the engine's special personality; no lack of determination.

I'll stop at Chilliwack. And tomorrow have an hour or so to wrap things up before the end.

It was right along here somewhere, those kids were murdered. We read about it. They haven't caught the killer, or hadn't when I left home.

It's wet again on the highway. I put fresh batteries in the recorder this morning at Lake Louise. Mechanism may be worn. When I turn it on there is a long delay before it records, and, when I replay, the beginnings of sentences are missing.

Strangely suspended between the whims of two machines, both of which I ask no more than that they see me through to Vancouver. And if they do, I'll do what I can to restore them.

Driving now past Bridal Falls. Canoe tripping in Temagami, there is a circuit we used to call The Trout Streams, with a whole series of waterfalls. The most memorable of them is Bridal Veil. Somehow, knowing its name always adds to its impact; so much are name and place together in my mind that I can hear the water crashing against the rocks and see the splash leap across the pool below, all in the syllables of the name.

It's impossible to separate clouds from the sky in the direction of the setting sun. Soon it will be entirely dark. The deep colour of night is already looming close behind me, but I've arrived in Chilliwack. I'm going to find a motel for the night.

● ● ●

Morning light of the sixth day. The sun is bright behind me. The clouds gather overhead and reach down in front to meet the flat earth of the river valley that stretches between me and Vancouver, an hour's drive at most.

[132]

I feel apprehensive this morning. The car has stalled twice already and I'm still within Chilliwack city limits. The steering wheel shakes with the effort of the engine to get itself together for the last leg.

I didn't think to change that front right tire this morning. There's no point, really. I'm almost there.

It promises to be a fast drive all the way.

On the phone last night Ginny told me UBC called wondering where I was. I woke up during the night several times, horror-stricken that classes had started the beginning of last week, started without me. When I got up I knew that wasn't right, of course, but for reassurance I searched through the various correspondence I've had with the Department — and couldn't find anything with the date on it. Surely someone told me September 12th.

Julie said she's written me a letter already. It should be waiting for me, although knowing the Postal Service I might easily beat it there, by car; she mailed it last Saturday, the day I left.

Leaving Chilliwack.

The highway here is utterly level. Unlike the prairie stretches, it doesn't plummet dead ahead, but snakes urgently around various obstacles, most of them unseen, guessed at, bends in the river, clusters of buildings, a road designer's fear of uniformity. The river plain extends left and right to hills that suddenly rise upwards, yawning great lummoxes, heads lost in the clouds.

Two ranges glowering at each other across a plain. I drive between them, almost smug.

Visibility, fading.

Everything has faded now except the earth and sky which merge and close around me. Pavement drifts towards me, leaps suddenly, falls short, sweeps underneath in a vacuum rush, fades behind me. I have the sense of motion, the idea of it, but no real evidence that I am getting anywhere.

ten

My eyes slip over shattered bodies of animals on the road. Occasionally, as now just past, my vision briefly is impaled by the grisly display and I have to stifle retching and shift my mind away, frightened that it will make unbearable connections.

Yesterday I had more to say, and drove less, than any other day on the road.

The recorder problem was the batteries, after all.

Driving now some thirty miles out of Vancouver, I could as easily be on Highway 401, driving towards Kingston; the scenery is still clouded over, the vegetation almost identical. I'd be home in half an hour, there when the kids get home from school or, by evening, there to see them off to bed, if I were coming from farther away.

Laurie has had a special smell like fresh winter air since she was an infant and she has it still, you can breathe deeply against the nape of her neck and draw it in, a fresh alive smell.

Ginny sounded cool on the phone last night, self-possessed. There was an uneasiness between us when I left, as if to make the separation less a strain. It's been bothering me from time to time. I tend to see myself too much as Ginny sees me at any particular moment, as if my nature is determined by what she conceives it to be, how she perceives me. It's a form of tyranny I impose on her.

I popped miniature bars of soap from the motel into my shaving kit this morning, for Julie and Laurie. More a gesture than actually to give them, since it will be two full months at least. . . .

Wish Ginny and I had parted, not holding back. . . .

The land has gradually crumpled into contours again. The sky is clearing. Rolling down a long hill, now. The sign says Port Coquitlam. Ahead I can see a huge bridge over the Fraser.

I wish we were together still at Bellrock.

Rolling off the bridge now, around a banked causeway, still high above the earth. I'll be there soon; a lot to think about. Everything will be alright.

It saddens me to have this over, though, outside the normal flow of things. I've had a chance, by the sheer onward plod of driving alone across the continent, to see clock time collapse, to range through my life and draw discontinuous elements together in a pattern that has nothing to do with sequence, a lot to do with need. Perhaps I've subdued the hours for a while, expanded time to personal infinity: Grammy, my ancestral past; Ginny, the kids; childhood, Mom, Dad, Rich, Steve, Liz, Erry; Ginny and Julie and Laurie; ideas; motifs — family, variations on mortality; places — Bellrock, Port Carling, Temagami, Blair and Waterloo County, Fredericton, Montreal, Vancouver ahead of me, Bellrock.

Entering Vancouver now. Emerging from fiction. Time is snapping into line again. Soon I'll be in the real world, the trip behind me.

The first thing I should do before going out to the University is get a hotel room. Saves people the awkwardness of asking me to stay with them, or of not asking. I'll find a room and have some lunch, and then go out and see what's happening.

epilogue

Things change and stay the same. Julie and Laurie are now in high school. Ginny works as a Psychologist and I teach Canadian literature at the University of Ottawa, commuting during the term.

My father died less than a year after we returned from the West, and I realize the anomaly, now, of how little of him is in this book; but that is a different story. Lady and Troy and Paddy are dead, and Shadow, a bouvier who came after Paddy, is gone too.

We still raise bees, descendants of the ones we left during our year in Vancouver.

We have several purebred Morgan horses; Quietude is the pride of our immodestly named Bellrock Morgan Horse Farm.

We canoe-trip in the summers, nearby and farther north.

In the winter we ski; this year in four marathons we as a family covered 1165 kilometres.

[139]

We walk a lot, around home and farther afield.

We have a good wine cellar now. I collect Chateau Mouton and have some classics which I may never bring myself to drink.

We have travelled twice in Europe since the fall of '77, through the good fortune of my academic specialty.

We still live here: Bellrock, Spring, 1983.

erratum

Several years have slipped a digit in the text; but this isn't history, and the sequence is right.
Also, on page 129 gremlins changed my uncle's name from Fred to Tom. He was always, in fact, just "Uncle" to those closest to him.

J.M.

postscript

I would like to thank the following people for reading the manuscript and offering their comments, many of which have helped to shape the final text: Patsy Aldana, Elizabeth Clare, Bill Cockburn, Matt Cohen, Diane Creber, Don Gutteridge, David Helwig, Enid Lavin, Jack McClelland, Mary Moss, Barbara Seachel, Ian Underhill, Charis Wahl, especially Charis Wahl, Caroline Walker, and, of course, Ginny and Julie and Laurie.

This is a work of the imagination, no less than if it were untrue.

[143]